PETER'S G

A book for the Elderly

JANE SHERWOOD

Foreword by
W. M. FORD ROBERTSON, MD

SAFFRON WALDEN
THE C.W. DANIEL COMPANY LIMITED

First published by
The Churches' Fellowship for Psychical and Spiritual Studies
in 1973

This edition published in Great Britain in 1992
by The C.W. Daniel Company Limited
1 Church Path, Saffron Walden
Essex, CB10 1JP. England

ISBN 0 85207 259 7

Produced in Great Britain by
Ennisfield Print & Design, London

Contents

To

SIGNE TOKSVIG

Who suggested the theme of this little
book and whose helpful criticism did
much to shape its form.

Foreword

Real studentship is all too rare in psychic matters, alas, but because of Jane Sherwood's integrity, objectivity and self-sacrifice over many years, her automatic writings through her communicators are of real worth. This quality of work belongs to the realm of genuine research.

As a physician with special interest in man's mental constitution, and being also deeply concerned with that element that is called the transpersonal – man's soul and spirit – I have read *Peter's Gate* with admiration and relief that someone has had the insight to give such clear concepts of the hereafter to those who speculate about death with dread or, at best, with uncertainty. I should hope that the clergy will also recognise the value of the message this small but important book represents. It is one that will comfort many in the near twilight of life by reducing fear and removing the 'closed view' of what lies beyond those feared words 'the grave'. Many of us who have been deeply involved with suffering humanity have a certainty that there is an after-life and I am personally convinced that this is so.

Science, with its entire focus on the material, has its essential place. Nevertheless, as Jane Sherwood states 'more than half of our everyday activities cannot be covered by scientific explanation'. It is the non-material, intangible things that are reality for most of us, especially our emotions, drives and values, the latter giving purpose and meaning to life, and these have little to do with scientific learning. The concepts that such values as truth, beauty, justice, love and compassion are intrinsic to human nature, a part of the whole man, are, amongst others, the foundations of the modern transpersonal psychology; a number of psychologists now, as part of their philosophy and practice, affirm that we have a spiritual mode of being. There is gradual realisation that we are much more than our bodies and that there is a real I, an inner self that can guide and control our lives on this plane and is that which Christ promised survives death.

The author truly affirms that it is to our peril that we have so far failed to master the secrets of the mind and soul. The deep unconscious mind would not appear to consent to our coming to a dead end for those who listen to their inner self usually live on in serenity and good mental health as if reassured by good news. On the other hand, we all know the psycho-somatic diseases contributed to by the fear and conflicts of the conscious and subconscious mind. These may also undermine the functions of the brain, leading to depression or anxiety, hastening memory failure and our loss of grip on life. I would commend for your study Jane Sherwood's two previous books, referred to amongst others in the text, giving us a much better insight into our fourfold nature and how greatly this is tied up with both our present life and that which we may expect to lead after death.

In thirteen well-arranged and vivid chapters the author gives us the message of *Peter's Gate*; for example, how we can mature in outlook and relationships, on being friendly with loneliness, dealing with the experience of weakness and pain and how to be friendly with the young. In the early chapters she deals with our limited understanding and insight, with their dire effects on ourselves and our dear ones. She effectively hits the nail on the head time after time with a simple yet shrewd directness that penetrates deeply. To me it was a delight to read, particularly as it is shorn of all psychological technicalities. Only those deeply disturbed and warped in personality can fail to be awakened to the limiting effect of their fears and doubts about their future. As is so clearly pointed out in later chapters, we cling desperately to the known and loved, to contemporaries and places, sometimes in vague depression and despair as well perhaps as a crippling disablement of some kind. But suppose we came to realise with a feeling of greater certainty that beyond the grave we shall walk into a new and greatly expanded life, then surely the remaining years could become an important opportunity for preparation. With this vision and new hope every moment left to us should be precious, to be utilised to the full in enriching or correcting relationships at all levels and ages and in general always moving away from the personal, limited, selfish self and instead using the inner, real self, the soul infused with spirit, through which to contact others in love and understanding. What opportunities many of us miss to achieve the best possible ripening of the personality!

In Chapter Ten, taken from the depths of her knowledge, the fourfold nature of our body is described in a detailed account of what happens in the process of their separation when the physical body is dying. To many it will be most reassuring to understand the phases of demise and that what is distressing to the onlooker is not experienced by the one in the manifest last stages of leaving the body for the real personality has already gone. To provide further assurance Jane Sherwood gives four contrasting accounts of after-death experiences, obtained through her mediumship.

In the chapter 'Meeting and Parting' it is asked whether, if we accept the fact of survival, we can expect to find our relationships with those we have known to be unchanged. The author has reservations as well as encouragement to give on this point. What is paramount, it seems, is the *quality* of the earth relationship, for shams are unthinkable over there; they just do not work. To those who had a deep attachment based on affinity, with unselfish love and mutual respect and understanding, the joy of reunion it seems, will be far greater than we could experience on earth.

In the last chapter, 'In His Will is our Peace', she ends with a beautifully expressed and hopeful 'Amen'. If we obey His will it seems that we have worked *with* rather than *against* the creative love that moves in and through all things. Death will come then not as a foe but as a friend, for our destiny lies in the extent of our spiritual knowledge and growth.

W. M. FORD ROBERTSON

CHAPTER ONE

Under Sentence of Death

The summons has come. I have only a short time to live. Long ago I used to think 'at least I have twenty years more', then it shortened to 'ten years' and now the moment of realisation has come and I know that the time is short. This ageing body, already beginning to fail me, will respond less and less to my demands until it finally sinks into uselessness. Before long, I must expect to take a strange and solitary journey into the unknown and on this journey no one can accompany me. Kind friends will doubtless assemble to see me off but I must dare the departure alone. My unwilling feet are already on the slope leading down to the valley of the shadow.

So; a spark of life entered a body at my birth and this spark will flare out into the dark when I die. Birth and death; twin mysteries of the beginning and the end. A phrase comes back to mind: 'In my beginning was my end'. Words of ill-omen, for my days were indeed numbered from my birth and soon their tally will be completed. But what about the converse: 'In my end is my beginning'? The end itself a beginning? Dare I believe that the darkness of death will lift into the shining of a new day?

Even though they are thrust down and unacknowledged, some such thoughts must be in the minds of most elderly people. It is one of the tragedies of our

1

age that to such questions a hopeful answer comes to so few of us. It is surely the part of wisdom to face the challenge of our situation and find courage to look quietly into the face of death. Evidence that the soul does not just flare out into the dark has been accumulating for a long time and a belief in our survival of death need no longer be derided as merely wishful thinking. Reasonable people have good grounds for such a faith. The conviction that there is more in a man than the chemical and electrical mechanisms of his body is evident even to a little introspection; it is confirmed out of our everyday experience, since so much of our living is done in non-material terms. Strange intimations of another order of being, half-understood experiences of beauty and truth testify to the existence of an order of being which at times invades our dusty earth. Such intuitive experiences come to most of us at times even though we fail to understand them or give them credence. But they make us know that we are more and other than our bodies and it becomes possible to assume that the immaterial entity that is the real 'I' may survive the death and disintegration of the body. To come to this conclusion alters the whole perspective of living and dying. It means that now I *dare* believe that the darkness of death will lift into the light of a new day.

'For in that sleep of death what dreams may come . . . Aye, there's the rub.' If we do indeed survive can we make any guess at what awaits us in that new life? Scraps of Sunday-school lore about the hosts of the shining ones, golden harps and crowns and never-ending songs of praise come floating back from our childhood days. But this exotic dream of bliss hardly seems the right setting for our workaday selves; we cannot see ourselves fitting happily into such a world.

Other and more reasonable ideas come to us from modern sources. Many devoted men and women have trained and disciplined themselves until they have become sensitive instruments through which such information can come. Do not discount it as wishful thinking, moonshine or madness. There is a sober correspondence between the independent findings of many such workers in the field of psychic research, a coherence in their visions, a reasonableness in their conclusions. Many books are available,* some providing evidence of the survival of personalities, some building up pictures of this new life, others working to find a scheme of thought into which both our earth-knowledge and that which comes to us from this world beyond death can be fitted.

Shall we not equip ourselves with what knowledge is available? Here we are, inescapably face to face with two possibilities: we survive death, or we do not. If we do not, that is the end and what is all the argument about? But if we do survive, it can do no harm to investigate. There is at least a fifty-fifty chance that our research may stand us in good stead. If we are not convinced one way or the other, we may safely examine honestly what evidence there is. I am prepared to believe that an impartial consideration will at least lead us to accept survival as a working hypothesis. Taking this for granted, let us look at our life here and now. We shall have gained a new perspective because if death is not the end, the short space of life still left to us becomes far more significant. The concluding stages, far from being just a dull and undignified descent into nothingness, become the thrilling prelude to a new adventure in living. Old age takes on interest and importance, for we have much to do to prepare for this adventure.

Suggested Reading

The Enigma of Survival, Hornell Hart

Survival of Death, Paul Beard

Evidence of Personal Survival from Cross-Correspondences, H. F. Saltmarsh

The Road to Immortality, Geraldine Cummins
(Edited by Signe Toksvig)

Swan on a Black Sea, Geraldine Cummins
(Edited by Signe Toksvig)

Post Mortem Journal, Jane Sherwood

The Country Beyond, Jane Sherwood

The Imprisoned Splendour, Raynor S. Johnson

The Personality of Man, G. N. M. Tyrrell

The Psychic Sense, Laurence Bendit and Phoebe Payne

CHAPTER TWO

Intellect and Intuition

On our journey through life, the prospect of death has closed in our view of the future. The distant scene has been obscured by a barrier through which we have not been able to see. Now we have come nearer to it, the obstacle looms more threateningly. We feel the check, and it seems that having come so far and covered so much of our journey, we are ultimately to be defeated. What does it avail us if, having overcome so many difficulties, survived so many crises on the way, we are in the end to be lost?

> 'Out, out, brief candle!
> Life's but a walking shadow, a poor player
> That struts and frets his hour upon the stage,
> And then is heard no more: it is a tale
> Told by an idiot, full of sound and fury,
> Signifying nothing.'

To such a dusty answer our modern creed of materialism must inevitably bring us. We are asked to believe that however worthy and useful our lives may have been, however well we may have served our day and generation, death will blot it all out. We ourselves must face extinction with what courage we may; time will quickly obliterate our memory from the world of men. Many worthy and honourable men, striving to be faithful to a scientific-world view, declare that they are content that it shall be so. They

5

protest that a man's integrity will prompt him in any case to live out his life worthily. One can only respect such a courageous attitude, but the underlying fear of death is not so easily exorcised. Although the conscious mind may strenuously endorse such a belief, the unconscious is not so easily fooled. It does not consent to this dead end and will revenge itself on the so-valiant conscious mind in many insidious ways. It may attack the body so that ailments and psychosomatic illnesses develop. It may attack the mind; melancholic anxieties and fears will arise. It may attack the intellect; hesitations, loss of memory, failure of mental grip will result. In some way or another the unconscious will register its protest.

Yet if the scientific-world view which ignores all but the material aspects of life is once accepted, what else can an honest man believe? He feels that his integrity is at stake; he fears that hidden wishes for survival may lead him into wilful delusion. So he takes his stand on verifiable fact and so must regard the death of the body as annihilation. We leave him, poor honest man, up against his prison wall. He will not look for the key which would unlock its door.

The scientific view is after all true to its own premises in ignoring all but material entities. The success it has had in charting and analysing matter down to the smallest unit of the parts of an atom has blinded us to its confessed limitations. Because of its successes in the mechanical field, we expect it to be able to account for every part of life but by its self-imposed limitation to what can be weighed or measured in material terms it makes such a feat impossible. More than half of our everyday activities cannot be covered by any scientific explanation. All the immaterial things that make the reality of living and without which we should not care to go on living at all must be ignored on a purely scientific view. What of the varied emotions that colour and vitalise all our doings? What of the strong emotional drives that give purpose and meaning to life? What of beauty, truth and love; the eternal values that are basic to human existence? What of thought itself and the rich life of ideas? We shall be asked to believe that these are merely chemical by-products of processes going on in the brain cells, surely too simple an explanation. It carries the assumption that a chemical change causing a vibration in a nerve is the same thing as a thought. But a vibration is *not* a thought. What, or who, interprets it as a thought? We are trying to compare two things that exist on different planes of being and which simply cannot be proved to be equal. There is obviously a fallacy here, a missing term to the equation. The materialist forgets that even to support his own thesis he has to use the immaterial entities that his theory denies.

These immaterial elements in our lives have real being. They are not just chimeras. They are the moulders and makers of our characters, the deeply felt core of our being. We believe that they have an independent and indestructible existence. The amount of evidence for survival has mounted up in recent years. There are many books that describe the experiments and findings of research in this field. We do not propose to cover here the ground so ably charted by others. We believe that the human body is not the simple chemical structure assumed by the materialist. There is a reasonable hope that more thorough research into its complexities will reveal its true nature as a four-fold structure: a physical body allied to a 'life' body and these animated by an emotional and a spiritual form interwoven with the others and yet capable of existing in its own right. A study of sleep, dreams, trance states and other unusual modes of consciousness* supply us with evidence of the independent working of these modes of our complex being at times when they are not fully combined to produce our accustomed consciousness.

Meanwhile the conviction is growing that science cannot be expected to account for more than its own restricted field of human experience and that a great deal remains outside its orbit. The essentially human and significant part of life can never be interpreted in its material terms. Here is the area calling out for research by the skill and patience of future men of genius. Science has mastered an amazing knowledge of the external world and this has given us an unprecedented power over nature. But to our peril we have failed to master the secrets of the mind and soul of man. We know a great deal about his body, but this complex being is still a mystery.

While we await discoveries in this field we may do worse than consider some of the conclusions reached, not by scientists nor even by psychic researchers, but by men and women of intuitive power – poets, mystics and seers. They have the right to speak with authority of that inner world of reality to which science is blind. They are citizens of this country;

*See my *Four-fold Vision*

the inner world of the spirit is their home. They cannot doubt its existence because it is part of their living experience. In the Kingdom of Heaven there is no need to argue about immortality; it is a state of being which partakes of eternity and so knows no doubt as to its inclusion in it. Poets, seers and prophets have lived in this state of eternal life here and now and they know it as a fact of experience. To speak to them of death as extinction would be an absurdity.

So Emily Bronte, out of her rich, deep, inner knowledge wrote:

'There is no room for death,
Nor atom that his might could render void.'

and Rupert Brooke, younger in self-knowledge, yet sees man as an 'exile of immortality'.

Henry Vaughan the Silurist knew these 'realms of light' into which his loved ones had gone and saw that death was no enemy, but a friend:

'Dear, beauteous Death! the jewel of the just,
Shining nowhere but in the dark,
What mysteries do lie beyond your dust,
Could man outlook that mark.'

Edward Carpenter, that wise nature mystic asks:

'When all life has been rich in experience
Shall not death be rich in experience also?'

and he tells us;

'Death is the law of eternal growth.'

Our thinking is so shut in by 'custom and supposed necessity' that we are in danger of becoming the prisoners of our own vaunted cleverness, as though our cunning mental tricks could interpret the vast meanings of the cosmos. So we brick ourselves up in our own prison and it takes the dreaded end of all things, death itself, violently to release us. But why wait for death? Our prison only waits for us to open the door and escape. Even if we are too blind and obstinate to accept our own release, we shall have to emerge when death knocks at the door.

Fixing our eyes on our inescapable fate, we may learn to see it as no blank ending, but a natural and necessary part of a rounded-off lifetime. We shall see it and accept it in proportion to the whole. This will involve nothing less than a complete change of attitude, a turning towards a different point of the compass so that light falls in unfamiliar ways on the familiar landscape. Once we have attained this vision we shall find it is an opening from which more of the way onwards is to be seen. Viewed from this point, death becomes just a feature of the wide-spreading landscape ahead. In so far as we see beyond it, it takes its rightful place; it marks, not an end, but a beginning. The path beyond is lit up with sunlight.

Moreover, this present phase of our journey which had seemed only the tired prelude to a dead end, now takes on a different aspect. It *matters*. Before, it had begun to lose meaning; the shadow of the end had fallen across it and robbed it of all colour and light. Value had gone out of things, leaving us with only a few small and ignoble satisfactions as compensation. We have been like people who know they will be forced to leave a familiar house where all the great experiences of life have come to them, where they have known happiness and sorrow, joy and pain. Its rooms are rich in memories, its furniture, shabby now, was once bright and gay and each piece carries associations with those friends with whom life has been shared. Now the roof of the house begins to leak, there are cracks in the walls, and we shall have to leave it. But because we have not known where we are going when at last its door closes behind us, we have been the prey of dread and doubt. Our thoughts have clung desperately to the known and loved and have refused to look into a dark and uncertain future. Inevitably we have restricted our anticipation to the short time we can hope to remain. But if, when we have to leave our shabby and no longer comfortable house, we can know that we shall walk out into a new and fuller life, how the aspect of things is changed! The dull and shadowed remnant of life in the old house has become an important opportunity for preparation for a splendid future and we are startled to think how short a time it may be. We need now to use every moment of it purposefully, for there is much to be done. Along with the new vision of the country beyond some of the vigour and enthusiasm we need has returned. The new perspective has brought with it a new attitude. Hope, faith and expectancy revive as we begin to prepare for the shining future. We are done with the vague despair, the listless inertia which had begun to paralyse us.

A script received by Mrs Isabel Ryder of California reads: 'There is a certain humor in your contemplation of the inevitable transition of death, because to a very large degree you have made it already. You are now functioning with the tools and to quite an appreciable degree with the organs of the larger life. What we visualise as a real possibility is a kind of growing transparency in the sheath of the physical body. Rather than acting as an obstruction it may become lighter, less dense, more translucent, so that the organs of the etheric or resurrection body can operate through it. This is a normal openness that might easily come to many in old age. If you can show and teach that old age is itself an important stage in the transition, you will do much to overcome the fear of death.

'Given the natural openness of this period many persons would be aware directly of life's ongoing were they not culturally conditioned to fear and hold back. Think what it would mean if the aged could be provided with an environment of quiet peace and harmony where they were encouraged to open in themselves the wider awareness of the new life towards which they are pressing. Can't you see how this would transform what we have called 'death' into a passage looked forward to with anticipation of joy and great expansion of life's meaning? Can't you see how this would change the last period of life? The reverberations then would flow down to all the stages of life and change many patterns and goals. If all life has been lived courageously and is seen to be a great adventure in experience, will not death be seen as another great experience?'

CHAPTER THREE

On Attaining Maturity

We have, then to be ready to say goodbye to our old home and to prepare for a new future. In what way can we best do this? We; our essential selves, are all we shall be able to take with us when we depart. What is this 'self' of ours really like and how can we make it more fit to bear us onwards into a new mode of living?

We have a lifetime of varied experiences behind us. In aspect, at least, we are 'grave and reverend Signors'; but have we really reached maturity or are we still adolescents masquerading as grey-haired dignitaries? In the real sense of the word 'maturity' has very little reference to the fulfilling of a number of years of living, or of having attained a ripe old age. Maturity can only be said to be reached when all the potentialities of our nature have been realised; it may, therefore, come early or late in life, or even not at all. The reaching of this final stage of development is indeed quite rare, especially in this age of specialisation. Circumstances, the choice of a career, the necessity of earning a living and the limitations of that chosen course, will all have exerted their pressures on us to prevent an all-round development. We have probably used only a fraction of our real talents; we may indeed be unaware of their extent and of the neglected part of our total being.

Psychology has discovered that each one of us has a complex nature of only part of which we can be aware. There is in each of us a light side and a dark side; an undeveloped as well as a developed nature. The so-called dark side is mainly made up of those unwanted parts of our nature which we have had to suppress in favour of our more useful powers, but although repressed, these things are not dead nor even sleeping but are alive and active in the unconscious. We avoid realising their presence because they are powerful and make us uneasy, but they are all part of the total personality which needs to be given a chance to develop fully. The so-called 'dark side' is not necessarily bad; in fact, it may contain much that is of value to our full development.

It seems also to be a proven fact that in middle age, when the difficult climacteric is reached both for men and women, there is a tendency for the buried parts of the personality to make a strong bid for a place in the sun. They rise dangerously near to the surface of consciousness and upset the emotional balance. It is then that we are given a chance to re-orientate our lives and to balance anew an often lopsided development. This welling up of impulses of which we have been unconscious sometimes causes such stress in the mind that what we euphemistically call a breakdown is suffered. Frustrated emotional drives of great power well up into consciousness to bewilder us. To fight these and attempt to repress them again is to make our condition worse. The cure may be, not to struggle back to the *status quo* but to accept the suggestions of new lines of development and so eventually to achieve a greater measure of wholeness.

Here great courage is needed, for the emergence of unconscious forces often creates panic in the conscious mind which is appalled at the strength and violence of these impulses. If we are strong and brave enough to remain in control, to study and to use these new impulses our life may take on fresh and richer meaning. We need then, to look well at what is emerging and decide whether it has value for our life. If we are fortunate enough to have the help and guidance of a qualified counsellor at this stage we shall benefit from it more safely but even lacking the wisdom of such a friend we shall find that the symptoms themselves contain the right suggestions for a cure.

Our conventional friends will probably be uneasy unless we go back to the pattern of our previous behaviour. We shall be subjected to the pressure of the ordinary. How great this pressure can be, reinforced as it is by our environment – houses all made to pattern, furnishings alike, clothes as the fashions dictate, the daily round of business, drinks with friends, bridge, golf, 'keeping up with the Jones' – one has only to step out of line to be made to feel the full weight of the safe and ordinary. So we may expect to be exhorted to push the unusual out of sight, bury it and go on with the crowd as before. What we are really being urged to do is to re-bury the essential self which is never ordinary nor conventional. We shall be on the road to a sterile self-impoverishment if we yield.

The parable of the talents may be over-familiar to

us, but it is very relevant to our problem. There was a man, we are told, who was given a talent to use, and who dug a hole in the ground and buried it safely therein. This is what every one of us has done. We all have rich talents, rich powers, hidden in the unconscious part of our being, but what we have thrust down into the darkness is not inert gold but something alive and struggling beneath the mould. It demands to be given its chance of expression in the sunlight. Moreover, we are impoverishing ourselves. We lack the special powers this buried talent might bring to us; we are incomplete without it. So when middle age comes and the pressure of ordinary living begins to slacken off, we have a chance to pause, take stock and re-orientate our lives so that we may use some of these hidden potentialities.

This then, is the time to 'break out', to forsake the familiar pattern of living and bring a new vision to bear. But we shall need first to give time to serious self-study. Let us not be frightened off by the parrot-cries of 'morbid introspection' or 'egotistical imaginings'. Perhaps for the first time in our lives we have leisure to study this complex self of ours. Complex it certainly is and not the simple duality of body and soul. There seems good evidence that a more accurate analysis would prove that we have a purely physical body actuated by a body of sensation, working in co-operation with an emotional form, and these all interpenetrated by a spiritual mode of being. This analysis will be more fully discussed in a later chapter.

Meantime let us think steadily of the life we are now leading and try to find out why we are not satisfied with it. Let us think back to the things we have wished to do and have been prevented from doing by the stress of events. What of our early dreams, dreams that had to be put aside perhaps because of the harsh necessity of earning a living, perhaps under the pressure of disapproval by others? Now that the pressure is slackening some of these dreams may still be possibilities. For once, let us encourage ourselves to be thoroughly discontented with the present state of affairs. Even Shakespeare knew this mood:

'Wishing myself like one more rich in hope,
Featured like him, like him with friends
    possessed,
Desiring this man's art and that man's scope,
With what I most enjoy the least content.'

As a result of this excursion into the past and its comparison with the present we may be able to arrive at a steady view of our real capabilities. We can judge coolly how many of our early dreams are really worth while and practicable in the present. We may then be able to break the spell of the ordinary and to release some of the neglected powers of our own nature. This is to make a new start in this life and to forward our preparations for the next. Let us not be paralysed by the thought that we may have only a few years to pursue it. We can go forward with our new development as though a long and joyful experience still lies before us. For we are not working for the sake of a few remaining years here; we are working for an eternal future and that it may be a joyful one.

This middle-age 'conversion', the opportunity for which comes to most of us as the great compensation for the trying re-adjustments of the climacteric, has critical importance for our true development.

Perhaps you have always been a social and gregarious person, an extrovert in our modern jargon. You would describe yourself as a lover of your kind. You need to have people about you all the time. You fear and dread aloneness. Silence oppresses you and you feel you must rush into speech no matter what about and if there is no one to speak to you turn on the radio or go out quickly to find a companion. You are happiest in a crowd, all of you talking, laughing, gossiping and making a jolly noise together. No matter what you chatter about so long as there is the sense of warm togetherness and of excitement and heightened being. It is easy to you to accost the stranger and to enter into talk with him, to relate your own life history or to listen to his. You are a kindly, friendly person and you wear your heart on your sleeve.

All this is good and healthy, but even here all is not well, for why this dread of being alone, why this fear of silence? Is there something buried underneath all the jollity that is trying to be heard? Are you so afraid of it that you must perpetually run into distractions of noise, talk, the gramophone, the radio? Is it possible that unless you see yourself constantly in the mirror of other men's regard you cannot feel real yourself? What is this void at the heart of all your good fellowship that frightens you whenever you cannot bury it under chatter or activity? There is a grave at the heart of your life and in it is your lonely and neglected self, never acknowledged, clinging to an impoverished life and terrified of oblivion; 'buried alive'. It is this that stirs in the silence and frightens you with its own fear. It is this that tries to speak in the solitude and sends you panic-stricken back to the herd.

But suppose, now that you are re-considering your life, you decide to stop running away from your buried self and gather the courage to acknowledge its existence? Suppose you check your dread of loneliness and sit quiet and deliberately give it a chance to speak. Suppose you seek the silence to hear what it is feebly trying to tell you? Suppose you read more, think more, ponder some of those abstract ideas you have always scorned in favour of 'real' satisfactions, that begin to seem now not so real as you had supposed. Indeed, have you not mistaken the shadow of life for its substance? Who *is* the madman, you or the mystic?

As you cultivate this neglected inner life your compulsive need for the stimulation of talk, of company, of noise and distraction will lessen. You are beginning to be a real person in your own right and not a doubtful creation which must constantly reassure itself by seeing its image in the minds of others. You will be fascinated to discover the depth and richness of experience in this new kind. As you allow your own inner life to develop so your love and understanding for others will deepen. You will see them now not only as pleasant companions but as living souls with unacknowledged hungers and needs such as you are discovering in yourself. You will no longer listen only to the words they speak as you used to do; you will begin to be aware of the questing spirit over which the words are a mere froth, a spume of disguise. There are lonely souls all around you, prisoners fretting in a wilful captivity under all this chatter and gaiety. Perhaps when you have begun to liberate your own captivity you may be the means of opening the prison doors for others.

On the other hand, perhaps you are introspective by nature, an introvert to whom the inner life of the mind is all-important. You too have buried an essential part of your nature and it needs to be given a chance to develop. Concentration on yourself may have made other men seem shadowy and unreal to you and your world has become a small and self-centred one. You have to break out of this prison of the self, this mini-world, into a larger sphere of action. You need to study your neighbour and try to find out what makes him 'tick'. You are half afraid of him, you lack faith in his goodwill and so you have turned your back on him. Lack of confidence in your world has been largely the cause of your self-centred attitude. Now, difficult as it may be, you have to get out and about among folk. You may plead shyness and the painful embarrassment it causes you. But shyness is only an insidious form of conceit. Do you regard yourself as 'sensitive'? What makes you think you are unique or specially interesting for this reason? Many of the apparently bluff and hearty souls you meet are equally sensitive and are merely putting up a defensive façade. So get over this affectation and take your chance of being hurt. What is hurt is your self-image, your vanity. So if you are hurt, keep it to yourself; it is no matter for pride but simply a measure of your own littleness. Open your eyes and your understanding, open your

heart and accept fully the richness of human relationships and the privilege of belonging to the human
family. You will still be an introvert; no one can take
from you your inner experiences, your intensely
intuitive mode of thinking and of feeling.

But these can now be put at the service of others
and can illumine your understanding of and sympathy with them. And what can you be at, keeping
this rich store of thought and inner experience to
yourself? Do you not realise that the world has great
need of it, that it is dying for want of it? Go among
men, open the secret storehouse of your mind as
occasion offers or as need becomes apparent. Be
prepared to use all that you have and are in the service of man. The more you open out to others the
less will you be a slave to yourself. The generous,
giving side of your nature will begin to expand and
thrive and will bring you warm satisfaction and
release you from the prison of self-centredness.

I have cited the cases of the extreme extrovert and
introvert, but most of us have natures somewhere in
between these two extremes. We still need to study
our limitations and try to exceed them. The man of
his hands needs to cultivate his thought life as well;
the intellectual to discover the satisfaction of making
and doing with his hands; the sceptic to examine
afresh his recoil from faith and to find out why he is
kicking against the pricks; the statistician or mathe-
matician to explore the worlds of art and music; the
housewife absorbed in domestic problems to open
her mind to the wider world of politics, literature and
the arts. We have a pernicious habit of sticking labels
on people: 'artistic', 'clever', 'practical', and so on

and we are too ready to accept the labels we have had pinned on to us and to allow ourselves to be limited by them. But no one of us can be summed up in a neat little label. We all have unguessed-at potentialities, many of them still undeveloped. Let us have more faith in ourselves. Tear off the foolish label and prove that you are much more than it described.

Each step taken along the road of self-discovery and self-development will bring us nearer to a true maturity. We shall need courage to face some of our discoveries. If we are honest we shall find that many of our actions are not so fair and beautiful as we thought. They have sometimes been motivated by mean and unworthy feelings which we have dishonestly translated into praise-worthy and noble ones. We shall perhaps be chagrined to find that many of our most unselfish and generous gestures have had as their motive a desire to be regarded by our friends as noble characters, and were only secondarily done to benefit others. We shall make many such discoveries as we scan the past and try to see ourselves truly in the present, and it will take some fortitude to accept ourselves as imperfect characters nor to be unduly depressed at our lapses. We shall find that the recognition and acceptance of our faulty selves will strengthen us, weaken the bad impulses so that we shall not be unconscious of them nor so much at their mercy as before. To see, to recognise and to accept one's dark side is to let in the daylight and to take from it its mystery and power. Moreover, some of this power will now be at the disposal of the conscious part of our minds and with an accession of strength many of our anxieties and fears will be seen to be groundless. There is joy, too, in the renewed confidence and spontaneity we shall gain, so the difficult search for a true maturity has great reward.

There is a further secret of development which is revealed to us only as we discover the heights and depths of human experience. It is as though in the unbearable intensity of great joy or great suffering some new power of the spirit is forged. If in the moment of stress we can consciously grasp and claim this new gift – the pure gold refined by the fire of terror or ecstasy – we shall be the richer ever after. It may be that when the emotional being is thus driven into almost unbearable intensity there is distilled from it a precious new quality of shining spiritual power. Only the courageous soul can benefit from this marvellous alchemy but it is to be noted that in a lesser degree every emotional experience can be profitable if it is accepted, consciously fixed in the mind and 'fed back', as it were, into the essential being. All the shining moments of our lives, all its sorrowful ones as well are for our enrichment if we can appropriate them in this way, but if grief dribbles away in self-pitying tears and joys flit by without being held they pass and we lose the power they might have brought to us. The emotional life developing in and through the diversity of our human experiences, gathers up its growing harvest of meaning to feed the spirit. The more intense and consciously felt is this inner significance of events, the richer food it provides for our growing spiritual bodies.

'Is your present experience hard to bear?
Yet remember that never again perhaps in
all your days will you have another
chance of the same.
Do not fly the lesson, but have a care that
you master it while you have the
opportunity.' *

Looking back over our lives we can probably see
how often we have let this precious element of
meaning soak away in tears or sink into the limbo
of forgetfulness. I believe that even so we can recall
in memory and relive these crises of experience so
that we find and appropriate from them the meaning-
ful values which at the time we missed. It is natural
to us all to avoid suffering when we can; some of us
are equally afraid of great joy or of any outstanding
experience which upsets the even tenor of our days.
In this we are wrong. Those are beloved of the gods
who have plumbed the depths and scaled the heights;
they are like the man in the parable who was given
ten talents and who used them to the utmost. For a
peaceful life the Greek maxim 'Nothing too much'
is no doubt a wise one but for the triumphant enrichment of the spirit one must have explored the
full range of our human fate and have learned how
to make spiritual profit out of every happening. So
if life has buffeted you, bruised and shaken you,
lifted you to pinnacles of joy only to dash you broken
to the ground again, rejoice. You are being given
opportunities of enrichment which are for ever missed
by the calm, placid souls whose path through life
seems so enviably easy.

---
* Edward Carpenter

CHAPTER FOUR

Making One's Soul

Recognising then, that the stresses of active life, the responsibilities of family, business and social life are, and need to be, the interests of our early and middle years, we are realising now that when the age of retirement comes there should be a shift of interest, a definite attempt to cultivate the neglected side of our nature. It is here that our attitude to religion becomes important. For many of us nowadays religion has come to be remote from our interests, something that we can ignore as unnecessary in our full and busy lives. The church stands where it always stood and some few people enter it but we go past the door without giving it a thought. If challenged we may take our stand on our steady principles, on our goodwill and amiable intentions and assert that these are enough. Certainly they are much, but now that we are really facing the future and the inescapable transition of death, can we be quite so sure about it? To dismiss the whole world of the numinous, the holy, with a facile scepticism is just not good enough; we know that we cannot continue to escape in this fashion.

Does God exist? How can I be sure? How much of the usual Christian doctrine can I accept? If we have honestly faced our own natures we shall have discovered that there are depths in us which we have not previously suspected. Surely there must be depths in the very nature of things to correspond with them. Besides, if I have found in myself that deep and secret centre of my own being I shall know without any argument that I touch something here which has kinship with God. The kingdom of heaven within *can* be found and experienced by any one of us and then we shall know of a certainty that God is to be found there. We are not all born mystics and this conviction may not be formed in us easily. Much quiet meditation and steady effort to still the busy chatter of thought may be needed. This is a discipline we can all follow, but in the search for an experience of the presence of God many men and women have been content to devote a lifetime. We can all begin to follow the discipline of meditation which is not the exercise of conscious thought, but depends on the stilling of that thought and the calling into play of the deeper power of intuition. This will develop in us a growth of the spirit and by its aid we shall find what we are seeking. Because a process of growth is involved we cannot expect to call such an experience into being overnight, but now in our leisure we have the opportunity to work and wait. So, if the will is truly set on this quest sooner or later we shall succeed. Then we shall have the only unshakable proof, the proof based on living experience. The faint and flickering inner light of our spirit will glow the stronger as it responds to its mighty source. We can reach this faith by no intellectual process, but we shall prove it on our pulses as unmistakable, immediate, experience. Let us keep steadily before us that great saying: 'The kingdom of heaven is within you' and never rest until we have realised it in our own lives.

Our trouble has been perhaps, that we have tried to think of God as somewhere 'out there' in the limitless universe of space. Here imagination is defeated. It was easier to believe in a heaven in the skies when we knew less about them. Now the mind is daunted by the unimaginable distances of cosmic space. Are we to envisage a God of this small earth? Of the whole solar system? Of the immense galaxy itself, or of the illimitable outer spaces with other and mightier galaxies? On and on in dizzying progression. Our finite minds reel and faint before such immense concepts.

> 'Not where the wheeling systems darken,
> And our benumbed conceiving soars! –
> The drift of pinions, would we hearken,
> Beats at our own clay-shuttered doors.' *

Our earthbound minds will always be staggered and defeated by efforts to envisage a God 'out there'. We are using the intellect to solve a problem that is amenable only to intuition – a spiritual mode of understanding. Only this God-given power of our nature is capable of apprehending that God who is a spirit. That God exists as the active principle in all being from the atom to the farthest star may be a formulation which our intellect can endorse, but it is powerless to move our spirit or to engage our loyalty. We may be thankful that we have this direct intuitive approach and that we need not despair because our *minds* are inadequate to such a vast conception.

To many people the concept of two kinds of truth

---

* Francis Thompson

is difficult. There are the truths that can be measured, assessed and accepted by the intellect, but there are also the truths that can only be found in actual experience and which have to be tested and accepted by the intuition. That is why all our efforts to measure and judge religious beliefs by an intellectual method are such grotesque failures. Religion is either experienced fact or it remains only belief or opinion. It is, of its own nature, only susceptible to the intuitive approach.

Most of us, however apparently irreligious, have a natural leaning towards some particular form of organised religion. Many lonely people find in association with a religious body much comfort and strength. In what has been a Christian country we are all more soaked in the spirit and tradition of Christianity than we realise and so for most of us some form of Christian church will be our natural spiritual home. We shall find differences in the creeds and practices of the various denominations and perhaps we shall be attracted and helped by one of these more than the rest. To many people the fellowship and support of a religious group is an essential part of the religious life, to others it may not be so necessary. But with or without the public profession of faith we need above all the inner experience of the Holy. Without this any outward profession will be rootless and impermanent. 'Is your religion rooted and grounded in spiritual experience?' Quakers ask themselves. If it is, then any superstructure of religious belief we build upon it will have unshakable foundations. Francis Thompson says: 'Know, for thou else canst not believe', and the direct awareness of the divine principle, the spirit, in the deep centre of our own being, answering to the unfathomable depths of the universal spirit, will enable us to *know*. Faith will be swallowed up in sight.

Whatever our religious experience may be, the purpose and goal of all religions is surely that they shall serve as means of growth; growth of the spirit. For however we may envisage the nature of God we have to admit that in all things that live there is manifest an inexorable law of growth and in this surely we must see an unchanging aspect of the will of God. Happiness as such, satisfied desires and realised hopes, good as these are, are not a necessary condition of growth. When we claim these things as our human rights we are sadly at variance with the realities of life. Blake said: 'Without contraries is no progression', and sorrow as well as joy, frustration as well as satisfaction, disappointments as well as fulfilment of hopes may be essential conditions for our healthy growth. The love of God is indeed 'broader than the measures of men's minds' and if this infinite love demands our growth for our own final well-being we must not grudge the cost. In the light of this divine demand we may see the increasing infirmities and trials of old age, even its very weaknesses and humiliations, as a final opportunity to attain to our full stature. We know that we have only a short time left; we know, too, how pitifully inadequate our spiritual development is. So the great concern of these later years is that the divine gift of the spirit may be given the conditions it needs for full and vigorous growth.

CHAPTER FIVE

Making a Friend of Loneliness

One of the saddest aspects of growing older is the gradual falling away of one's seniors and then of one's own generation. One by one the older members of the family go and the older among our friends die, and at last we lose the dear friends and lovers and companions of our own day. We find ourselves outliving our contemporaries and begin to feel that we are washed up on the banks of the river of life which is running merrily on without us. Our children and perhaps their children too, are absorbed in their own full and busy lives and however loving and sympathetic they may be we come to realise that we are really standing alone. In the old days there might have been a devoted daughter willing to give her strength and interest for our comfort but nowadays we quite rightly deprecate that sacrifice of young lives to maintain the warmth and comfort of the old. We have no right to expect it of our children and for most of us that solution of our aloneness is not to be thought of. So the stripping off of the genial companionships of our younger days may well leave us shivering in the bleakness of a real isolation.

Now that we are all living so much longer the problems are more widespread. The suffering caused to the old is sometimes acute. Many elderly people shut up alone in comfortless lodgings, poor and often cold and ill-fed, are in pitiable case. Even to them the deprivation of comforts and small luxuries is less of a hardship than is their desolate loneliness. Perhaps we ourselves, in seeking to alleviate their suffering may bring some ease to our own. Fortunately the problem is recognised and welfare workers are doing their best to bring some human comfort to such solitary ones. If our own state is less desolate we surely have much to be thankful for, but even so we shall probably have our own obstinate problem of loneliness.

There is a distinction we need to make between 'loneliness' and 'aloneness'. Loneliness is that forlorn and self-pitying state into which we may sink if we have always depended too much on other people to reflect back to us our own image – to make us feel real because they accept us as real. If we have always needed companionship to echo our random thoughts as we throw them out, to feed our casual interest with gossip about our neighbours, in a word, to create for us that light froth of human intercourse which has come to be necessary to us, then being alone will be a severe deprivation and will leave us diminished and hardly alive in any real sense at all. Then self-pity will flood in and we shall find being alone insupportable. We shall be like an addict who, when his special kind of stimulation is unobtainable, craves for his habitual dose. When such a person has solitude forced upon him he naturally becomes the prey of intense self-pity and this is the bitter pill in his cup of loneliness.

This is not to minimise the real suffering involved, but only to show that the suffering has a remedy. It is not unavoidable. The 'aloneness' may be inevitable but the 'loneliness' is not. Are we feeding our own misery with this bitter-sweet drug of self-pity? There is nothing more insidious and deadly in all the self-administered poisons we humans use. If we continue to indulge in it it will sap our strength, thin our blood and leave us a whining misery to ourselves and to our friends. Such of these as we still retain may well find that they cannot bear the reproach of our attitude. We can, and we must, snap out of it, and this is no easy thing to do. The constant dripping of the poison of self-pity will have weakened our will and the habit of repining will be difficult to break. We need to find a more positive approach and so weaken the habit from disuse rather than making a violent and perhaps futile effort to change ourselves. So let us look steadily at our situation. Here we are, no longer propped up by friends and companions but challenged to stand steady on our own two feet. Why not? We *can* do it. Straight and steady now and face the fact of aloneness. Take the self-pity out of it, test the strange but true feeling of the dawn of a new strength and take your first faltering steps alone. Soon you will have found your feet and can go quietly on. If self-pity creeps back again, as it may, do not despair but go on making efforts at independent action. Then begin to study 'aloneness' and the advantages it offers you.

If there is no one to support you, equally there is no one to check you. There is greater freedom to plan, to act and to live as suits us best. If this is the grudging gift of isolation, at least it *is* a gift. We may say that we don't want freedom at this price, but as we begin to adventure on our unaccustomed independence we shall begin to savour it and to feel some satisfaction in planning our days and directing our own actions. We may be chilled and discouraged at first by the absence of habitual duties to others, we may miss their demands and the obligations they laid upon us. But we have to test our strength and learn to step out alone with confidence. If we look around there will always be someone who needs our help. There will always be some ties of obligation and if we ourselves are friendly, new friends will come to us. There will be letters to write, small kindnesses to do and more leisure to see and respond to the needs of others. We shall be wise to encourage any new growth of interest in whatever direction it may lead us. After our first hesitating steps alone we shall cease to fear or repine and novel experiences will open up new vistas of satisfaction.

Another kind of freedom may dawn for us. We do not often realise how greatly our mode of thought is influenced by those with whom we live. Perhaps for years we have been taking our ideas at second hand and have unconsciously adopted someone else's attitudes to politics, religion, books and music. Now it may come to us with something of a shock that our thoughts about these things are gradually taking another form, that we are veering round to a different attitude, one that is easier to us because it is more natural. It is important not to fight this tendency to re-orientate our thoughts out of a mistaken feeling of loyalty to those we have lost. We have now a precious opportunity to be more fully ourselves, to think our own thoughts and to let our attitudes follow our natural bent.

All this is part of the rediscovery of the self which can be the special joy of 'aloneness'. One has perhaps never had time before, nor leisure from the press of other demands. Moreover, self-study has probably been condemned as morbid, self-centred and egotistical. But now this only concerns ourselves and we are free to be as introspective as we please. So, what kind of person am I? Now, perhaps, I can find out. How much of the usual 'me' that I have taken for granted is just a façade erected to satisfy other people? Well, meet a stranger, the unexpected and interesting person behind the façade. You may not altogether like what you find. It may not be so pretty as the façade, but it will be a great deal more real. It may not square with the ideals you have been taught to accept, nevertheless it will be foolish to panic and cover it up again. We all get shocks when we honestly face our real selves because we always find that we are both better and worse than our self-image. But now, in aloneness, you can afford to be completely yourself and if you are dissatisfied with what you have found, there is time and opportunity to alter it. One of the most valuable gifts of solitude is this encounter with the real self. You will find that if you shirk it it will be very much harder to come to terms with your aloneness because it will always contain the uneasy presence of a stranger, this stranger who is your real self.

There are many other compensations. Our life today is so often lived in a maze of noise and commotion. The city dweller is so inured to a ceaseless stream of sound that he is uneasy when it falls silent. The quietness of the country is no solace to him. He has to import his own kind of noise and so the blare of the radio ruins the peace of our woods, seaside and mountains. But if we are to become real friends with aloneness we have to learn to listen to the silence, to realise it as a rare luxury, an easement of tension, a balm for tired spirits. When, after an incursion into company, an evening of talk, laughter and fun we return to our solitary home and feel the luxury of 'coming home to ourselves', then we may know that we have finally conquered the bugbear of loneliness and our solitude will have become a benison.

CHAPTER SIX

The Experience of Weakness and Pain

With the coming of old age comes the probability of increasing weakness and the pains and penalties that may accompany it. Admitting, as I think we must, that the healthy growth of the immortal part of our being is our main concern in these later days, we must use this hazard of old age as wisely as we can. The essence and *meaning* of all experience is the food of our spirit and these are largely supplied by our emotions. Weakness and pain may make a dangerous attack on our emotional life, so, in effect, we have to find ways of avoiding anxiety and distress of mind even though our bodies may be suffering. So a little thought and a clear intention to keep physical suffering in its proper place may be useful.

Of course, we may be among those fortunate few whom death takes suddenly by the hand whilst yet they are in the full tide of living, but for most of us the years of encroaching weakness stretch ahead and we have to find ways of facing them with equanimity. Here, in parenthesis, one may say that as a rule women are better fitted to face these kinds of ordeals than men; feminine experience usually includes a good deal of practice in putting a good face on discomfort or suffering, whereas to a healthy male these things are unfamiliar and therefore the more disconcerting. However this may be, for most of us there will be periods of weakness and pain and although modern medicine will make things as tolerable for us as possible, there will still be plenty of calls on our courage.

Courage of a special kind is certainly needed. I am not of those who profess to find virtue in pain or that it necessarily has an ennobling effect on character. It all depends on how the pain is borne. If self-pity and bitterness are our reaction then the results of pain are bad. We have let the suffering of the body poison and corrode the spirit. If we can find enough courage to accept the pain without bitterness then the experience will strengthen and ennoble the spirit. Brave words, you may say; but what of the gripping of the whole consciousness in an intensity of pain that will not allow one even to *think* anything but naked, intolerable pain? How is it possible to accept this cheerfully? There is no answer to this awful question. The fortitude of the individual soul alone can deal with it.

There are, I think, certain techniques that can be learnt that will help to lessen the impact of pain. Some of them are simple and help most in cases of localised suffering. The pain, shall we say, is in the left arm. The natural tendency is to focus attention on that arm and on the pain in it. By thus doing we make sure that we shall experience the maximum degree of suffering. The arm is in pain and we identify with the arm and so suffer in thought as well as in body. To *think* a pain is to intensify it and to let it flood into every part of our being. After all, it is only a physical pain so are there any ways of keeping it in its own department? First, we need to relax the nerves and muscles we have tensed up to meet the attack. Deep and regular breathing will help us here. When we have thus quietened the physical panic that pain induces in the body we then have to deal with the emotions. Fear and resentment are the usual reactions to pain. We are afraid and so we fight the pain with anger. These natural feelings we have to replace by conscious acceptance. Cease to fight and give in to the situation. After all, it cannot be escaped and we shall only waste strength by bootless struggling. If we succeed in adjusting to it thus far, we can now try the third stage. Our efforts have at least given us something to think about beside the pain itself and now we shall try to detach from it still more. We need to make a determined effort to remove our attention from the painful area and deliberately focus it on another area of the body. Concentrate on something remote from the painful arm – perhaps on one of the feet – it doesn't matter where we transfer our attention to as long as we can tear it away from the pain-area. Now feel that foot, be conscious of its shape, size, of the separate toes, instep, heel and ankle. At first, attention will keep slipping back to the pain in the arm; with boring insistence it will try to claim our attention. Never mind. Recapture it and bring it back firmly to the foot again.

There are many advanced techniques for lifting the plane of consciousness right out of the physical realm altogether but these are too difficult for ordinary mortals to aspire to. Years of self-discipline and meditation are required before complete control of body and emotions can be attained. But simple devices such as I have described can be mastered and will at least reduce our suffering by an appreciable amount. The technique for us, then, is (1) relax the muscles, (2) dismiss fear and resentment and accept the pain, (3) deflect the attention to some other part of the body. This last can well be practised in hours of ease, learning to place the consciousness in any given part of the body and training thought to follow up any lines of interest arising from it. We cited a case where attention was to be focused on the foot. Arising from a consciousness of its shape, power and activity we may go on to think of walks we have enjoyed, dancing, games we have played and many pleasurable activities associated with our feet. Practice in this procedure will make it easier to use helpfully when the occasion arises. Apart from making it easier for us to bear, it is just possible that it will result in an actual lessening of the pain itself. One cannot guarantee this, but I know from experience that it can happen and that the pain thus ignored may actually lessen and disappear.

One is reminded of Gerald Heard's masterly summing up of the possible ways of meeting danger. The first reaction is to be frightened and run away. We see this in animals that rely on speed in flight for safety from danger. The second response is for fear to turn rapidly to anger and instead of running away we stay to fight. This aggressive response it typical of the carnivores. The third way of meeting danger is for fear and anger to give way to attention, curiosity and a reasoned response to the danger. This is, or ought to be, the typical human behaviour. How often we stop short at the purely animal reaction!

Pain is a threat of danger to the body; we would all run away from it if we could; we would fight it if this would do any good; we can and should be curious about it, attend to it and then use our reason in dealing with it. Being curious about pain has interesting effects. It shifts the centre of consciousness from the physical and emotional to the mental sphere of behaviour. It deflects attention from the mere fact of suffering and so lessens it. Certainly if we moan and groan and cry out that we can't and won't bear it, we shall take the heaviest possible punishment. If we can find the grace of acceptance we may diminish it and perhaps defeat it altogether.

It is easy to be glib when writing of this grim subject in time of ease. It might be more authentic if it could be written during the painful experience itself, but memories of acute suffering and a sympathetic imagination supply some evidence which may be helpful. We are such vulnerable creatures and just because of this, suffering has always been an inevitable part of the human lot. But we can wrest strength of spirit and serenity out of a courageous response to our situation, while craven behaviour can only result in moral and spiritual defeat. Questions about why there is suffering and why a good God allows it to torture our bodies may haunt us. All down the ages men have tried to fathom this mystery. My own guess is that it is bound up with the necessity for growth and that there are certain stages of development which can only be passed at such times of extremity. I have wondered whether in the last agony on the cross some such crisis was passed by Jesus. Albert Schweitzer hints at this in his *Quest of the*

Historical Jesus. But to answer the 'why' of suffering and to satisfy one's sense of justice perhaps we need the longer view of the theory of reincarnation. If in this present life we are re-learning lessons we refused or failed in in a previous lifetime; if we are paying in physical terms for some crime or cruelty committed then we might even rejoice in our present pain knowing that the debt was being paid and would hamper us no longer in any future lifetime. If the law of Karma operates, it does so in pursuance of divine justice used in the greater purpose of the growth and redemption of our spirits.

CHAPTER SEVEN

Relationships

Most of us, looking back over our lives and passing in review our youth and middle age, will find our minds following now one, now another of the many people with whom we have had close relationships. It is really this complex of relationships which has formed the pattern of our lives. We return in thought to our childhood and see again father, mother, brothers and sisters; and beyond them we remember the outer family circle of uncles, aunts and cousins. Then outside the home group we had school and college friends, workmates and business associates. All these and a great many more have influenced our thoughts and actions, have called out various emotions, have perhaps altered the whole trend of our lives. Each, as we recall them, is the centre of a system of emotions. Some we have loved, some hated; some have attracted us, some repelled us; some have inspired fear, others confidence; to some we have felt the liveliest gratitude, to others hostility. Just as we must have made our personal impact on their lives so our contacts with them have built up, moulded and modified our own character. For what is this but the end-product of our whole emotional life? Certainly all these relationships, happy or unhappy, are incorporated into our emotional being. They form the texture of what is in reality the most important part of that being. To a great extent we *are* this sum total of all our relationships.

So, as we contemplate them, thinking now of one, now of another, the appropriate emotions well up again; love for this one, sorrow for another, pain perhaps and anger, remorse for another, gratitude and admiration for others. In many cases our emotional response to these memories is mixed and puzzling, but whatever it may be, we shall convince ourselves that we have built up around our friends a living nexus of emotions. All these feelings are still alive and active in our inner life and we have learned with the years to live with this astonishing welter of contradictory emotions. Shall we try to realise that this is no vague assembly of mere 'feelings', but a real form of emotional substance which we have made for ourselves by our responses to all the personal relationships of a lifetime? On balance, would you say that the body thus formed is a happy and harmonious one, or would you have to admit, as most of us would, that it is marred by unhappy feelings of resentment and bitterness?

None of us is perfect and so we must all have to admit failures in some of our relationships. Perhaps we even have to realise that we have been guilty of crimes against love, hardheartedness, carelessness and irresponsible injuries to others. How are we to deal with the remorse which overwhelms us when we face ourselves in this light? We cannot just sweep all this past experience into limbo and say that it is finished with. It is far from finished since we have built it into our living souls. We cannot bury it in the past because it is still alive and active as a part of the structure of our being. It is very important for us to recognise this, because the body which will persist after death, the body in which we shall live on, is indeed formed of the very stuff of our emotions.

The physical body visibly remains on earth and is returned to earth. The etheric form with which we experience all the rich life of sensation – warmth, pleasant contacts – and all the other enjoyments of the senses, is shed soon after death. It is so closely bound up with the physical body that it does not long survive it. The life of the emotions, for which we use the old term, 'astral' form, is now the lowest mode of being remaining to us and so becomes our outward and visible form. Indwelling in it is the spiritual being, the essential meaning of our personalities, and the final and immortal part of our complex self. It gathers up in the form of meaning all the harvest of our life experiences in sensation and emotion and carries it on into eternity. Nothing is lost even though body after body is shed. The immortal spirit gathers it all up from mortality and takes it on in its own imperishable being.

'And seest thou not that except for Death thou couldst never overcome Death.

'For since by being a slave to things of sense thou hast clothed thyself with a body which thou art not master of, thou wert condemned to a living tomb were that body not to be destroyed.

'But now through pain and suffering out of this tomb shalt thou come; and through the experience thou hast acquired shalt build thyself a new and better body.'

So we shall have left our physical body behind, and

with it the etheric and we ourselves shall be now this emotional body which we have been building up during our earth-life. It is no wisp of formless spirit, but a body which will take on much the same form as our present one and will appear to us and to our companions as a solid and substantial one. It is a real body and in its make-up may be either beautiful and healthy or ugly and diseased according to the elements we have built into it.

The physical body has had its experiences in terms of sensations – hunger, thirst, desire and all the pleasures of the senses. These were due to the activity of the etheric body and these will be finished when we have shed the etheric body which produced them. What we shall have to live in and with now are 'feelings', and it is with these that we shall do all our experiencing. We can no longer think of 'feelings' as immaterial, intangible things, strictly private to ourselves and easily hidden or ignored. Our new body is permeated with its own light and colour and these fluctuate with every passing emotion, so that our feelings are now faithfully displayed for all to see. If they are healthy and happy emotions they will make our new bodies radiant with well-being; if they are painful and bitter they will show as actual blemishes, causing suffering to us and making others shun our presence. Our 'feelings' are no longer to be hidden or ignored, and lacking a material body to slow up their action they are far keener and more poignant than we can now realise. The substance of this new body, then, is already built and is still being modified by us during our lifetime. Is it going to be a healthy body or one that is poisoned and ill?

We shall be wise to begin now to think of our life of feeling in physical terms, since it will be the substance of our actual body in the new life. Then we shall be seen and recognised for what we are. We shall no longer be able to hide behind the mask of the flesh, covering dislike with a false smile, fear with bravado, indifference with a show of interest and disguising our real reactions with a smoke-screen of insincere words. Then, our dislike will show plainly in a dart of angry red, our fear will spread around us like a choking fog and our indifference as a dimming of our light. Candour will be compulsory and we shall have no defence but honesty.

We shall speedily realise, too, that this new body that should be so radiant and beautiful is alarmingly sensitive both to joy and sorrow, pain and pleasure. While we have the flesh to dull our reactions we can hardly envisage the poignancy of those feelings when they are free from the drag of the flesh and have to bear the stark impact of pure emotion. Our joys will be so enhanced that they will take the form of ecstasy and our painful feelings will become unbearably piercing. If we suffer from uneasy memories now what will the pang be like when we have to bear it in this keener form?

Let us not be too depressed. Many of our present emotional states can be improved, some of these unsatisfactory relationships can be put right now if we realise the importance of our feeling-life in time. If we can get rid of any lurking bitterness and substitute happier feelings, wrestle with our own obstinacy and try to heal some of the wounds we have made or forgive freely those we have received, there will be a corresponding change for the better in that all-important emotional body of ours. Although we cannot see it we can estimate fairly accurately what its present condition is, for it has even now the power to make or mar our well-being. It behoves us to set about our cure now, while we still have time, so that we may be spared the 'weeping and gnashing of teeth', which is the figurative way of describing the suffering we may be laying up for ourselves. Let us work at our cure now.

We have leisure now to give serious thought to ways of reconciliation and of better understanding with those friends we can still reach. But what of those who have gone ahead of us? Our response should not be a useless remorse but an effort to deal with our own side of the problem. That friend is still in existence, and he may have taken with him unhealed wounds of our making. If we can adjust our own attitude, admit our fault with sorrow, our repentance and desire to make amends will not be wasted. In some way it will help in his recovery as well as cleansing the poison from our own emotions. If, on the other hand, we are the injured party and can bring ourselves to understand and forgive, we shall be making recovery easier for our erstwhile enemy. Our own part is clear. We are out to cleanse and sweeten the whole of our emotional life, to substitute love and understanding for resentment and bitterness. So let us write that reconciling letter, visit again the friend we have shunned or offended, scan the book of the past with larger sympathies, and cancel for good those debts we have grudged.

CHAPTER EIGHT

Acceptance

The attitude to life which will help us most in our efforts to cleanse and clear the emotions is that of acceptance. The attitude of acceptance is good whether in the presence of danger or in the ordinary circumstances of our lives, the events that affect us and the people who make up our world.

Our circumstances are largely decided for us by our birth in a particular nation, class and family. Whatever these may have been we were wise if we accepted and built upon them, unwise if we wasted strength in resenting them or in envying those we thought better placed. Have we gone through life with 'a chip on the shoulder'? Some of us are inclined to excuse our faults and failures by carping at parents, early privations or just 'bad luck'. This endless drip of self-pity only weakens and impoverishes the will. The game of life is not to be played without its proper hazards and checks. These are the challenges we must accept and overcome or else confess ourselves beaten at the start. What has been our attitude to the given facts of our circumstances? As we look back we can see how often we failed to rise because we did not use difficulties as stepping stones but allowed them to trip us up. It is not too late for us to alter our tactics. Events may not move so fast for us now but they do move and we must go with them. Let us not be dragged unwillingly but keep alert and co-operative, taking as full a part as we can in the life of our world. So we shall accept our present circumstances and use all our wit and common sense in making them conduce to our progress.

The discipline of acceptance is most valuable as applied to our personal relationships. Have we ever considered how seldom we accept our friends for what they are without wanting to make them over again to our own pattern? Are we prone to a fidgety fault-finding; a deprecatory innuendo of 'if only they were like this', or 'if only they would do that'? Whatever the formula of criticism it shows plainly that we do not accept them. We allow ourselves to get irritated by people for no better reason than that they are not like our wonderful selves. So we consider it our duty to improve them, to set them right, to show them what they should do and how they should do it – a futile and exasperating effort. We carp at our friends because we cannot admit that they are as worthwhile in their own way as we may be in ours.

If we can drop our fault-finding and get the habit of acceptance we shall begin to see our friends in a different light. Here is the only, incomparable, John Smith in the world, here is that unique Tom Jones, admirable creatures, perhaps laughable, certainly lovable and always intensely interesting just because they are so different from ourselves. How many jarring discords might be removed if, instead of cheapening and depreciating our friends, we accepted and appreciated them! For our neighbour will quickly respond to our change of attitude and we shall begin to see him as he really is. Once the barriers of pride and fancied superiority are down we shall be able to see and love 'that of God' in him, as he in us.

Or is our attitude similar to that of those well-meaning but exasperating 'do-gooders' who are to be found at work among the distressed and suffering? The work they set out to do is beyond praise and yet somehow it is only accepted grudgingly and without gratitude. Edward Carpenter has understood the problem so well:

> 'Who are you who go about to save them that are lost?
>
> Are you saved yourself?
>
> Do you know that who would save his own life must lose it?
>
> Are you then one of the lost?
>
> Be sure, very sure, that each one of these can teach you as much as, probably more, than you can teach them.
>
> Have you then sat humbly at their feet and waited on their lips that they should be the first to speak – and been reverent before these children – whom you so little understand?
>
> Have you dropped into the bottomless pit from between yourself and them all hallucinations of superiority, all flatulence of knowledge, every scrap of abhorrence and loathing?
>
> Is it equal, is it free as the wind between you?
>
> Could you be happy receiving favours at the hands of one of the most despised of these?
>
> Arise, then, and become a saviour.'

Most of us have to look back with sorrow and shame to many spoilt relationships which might have been happy and rewarding if we had known and applied the rule of acceptance instead of resenting differences. How sad to realise now that we missed finding the shy and beautiful spirit that was hidden there awaiting our love and appreciation! True, we cannot retrace our steps and remorse is unavailing, but even now our change of attitude will modify our own part of the relationship, sweetening our thoughts of our friend and perhaps influencing him more than we can know. For we have a long future ahead of us and may yet be given opportunity to retrieve our fault. So regret and hope may go hand in hand.

Meanwhile our world will take on a 'new look'. For we are at last seeing the *real* people by whom we are surrounded and not the unhappy projections of our own critical spirit. How remarkable they all are! How intensely alive and individual! Even when their oddities make us laugh, it is a laugh of pure joy and appreciation. We are no longer surrounded by dull, glum and disagreeable people; they all seem to have had a face-lift. Lovely people, happy people, perhaps some who are tragic and sorrowful but still so gallant and cheerful. Thank God, too, for the fun and jokes and comedy of our human story. Accepting it all we can rejoice in the uniqueness and richness of all our friends in all their infinite variety.

If it is important that we should accept our fellows as they are, it is just as important that we should learn to accept ourselves. This is not the simple thing one might imagine, for who is there who really knows himself? In fact we come here to the hardest lesson of acceptance for we would all fain see ourselves as stronger, wiser, and far more noble than it is possible for us to be. Our inflated idea of ourselves leads us to set up false standards and impossible ideals of conduct. Our habitual picture of ourselves, cherished in the imagination as the 'real' self, is indeed rather different from the one our friends see. Here, built up during our lifetime is a beautiful persona, a lovely image of the self which we have set up for our own private worship. We even expect our friends to burn incense at the shrine and are surprised and hurt when they fail to do so.

When the stress of events betrays us into action which we feel is unworthy of this ideal self we are wont to excuse our lapse by explaining 'I was not quite myself' or, 'that wasn't really like me'. So we scourge ourselves in pain and disgust for our failure. The sense of guilt which torments so many people is often due to the discrepancy between the beautiful image and the actual person revealed by the testing of events. It is more gratifying to self-esteem to bewail lapses from perfection rather than to admit that we are not and never have been perfect. From the floods of self-justification or self-accusation in which we indulge when we are thus shamed the inference is plain: we are essentially perfect and this is nothing but an unaccountable lapse, but we are not really like that at all. We have all heard it, and we have all poured it out in our own defence. Faced with it in this form, notice how quickly we hasten to take the stick to ourselves before anyone else can reach it and to assert loudly that for our part we never imagined we were perfect, but . . . and following that 'but' we climb a little unsteadily back on to our pedestal.

There can be no peace for us until we have had the

courage and honesty to face our actual self. We have to look firmly at a creature of human clay, fallible, weak yet well-intentioned, headstrong, greedy and vain and perhaps selfish and lazy as well. *This* is oneself. The thing on the pedestal never had any real being. It is a false and hypocritical sham and the strain to make thought, word and deed correspond with that smug image has wrecked many people's health and nerves and has even upset their mental balance. It was some such lovely image that the Pharisee in the parable went up to the temple to worship. The Publican, on the other hand, was really facing his own contemptible self and not liking the look of it. Have we too the courage to see ourselves as truly as he did and to accept humbly what we see? Then we shall be set free from the bondage to the false persona and shall stop belabouring our poor selves because we cannot and do not rise to impossible standards of heroism and perfection. As we come to accept, we shall neither under, nor over-rate what we see, but shall value the good qualities as well as acknowledging the bad. Then we shall be able to deal faithfully with the false image and laugh at the silly smirk on its face and its air of superior wisdom. It will come down from its pedestal for good and all and we shall henceforth be free from its demands for worship and service. For this is the most secret and powerful of the idolatries which can ensnare the souls of men. The worship of the false self has been behind most of the cruel manifestations of human nature and is made worse because the self-worshipper is not conscious of his idolatry.

To accept oneself as one truly is does not mean a

smug self-satisfaction. When we can look steadily and see clearly we shall be able to say: 'Yes, I *am* like that; a very ordinary sort of person, neither wise nor good, neither clever nor unselfish. I don't like the look of myself at all but I will waste no time bewailing my shortcomings but will strive to amend them, forgiving myself as I hope that God forgives me. So I shall be free from the failures of the past to go forward and do better in the future.'

Of Mary Magdalene the author of the mediaeval *Cloud of Unknowing* says:

'And yet she wist well that she was a wretch most foul of all other and that her sins had made a division betwixt her and her God that she loved so much. But what thereof? Came she therefore down from the height of desire into the depths of her sinful life and searched in the foul stinking fen and dunghill of her sins; searching them up one by one and sorrowed and wept so upon them each one by itself? Nay, surely she did not so. For so might she sooner have raised in herself an ableness to have oft sinned than to have purchased by that work any plain forgiveness of all her sins.

And therefore she hung up her love and her longing desire in this Cloud of Unknowing and learned her to love a thing which she might not see clearly in this life; insomuch that she had oftimes no special remembrance whether that ever she had been a sinner or none.'

God knows the faulty nature of the physical and moral being which is myself. He cannot expect perfection from it nor will he blame it for its failure to realise an impossible ideal. Can we not trust God to be a realist? He surely takes no pleasure in continual wailing over failures nor in the waste of strength in fruitless sorrowing over our sins. Such an attitude betrays a self-centred obsession with what is for us an impossible standard of perfection. It is a disguised return to the idolatry we have foresworn. We only begin to realise the unfailing love of God when we cease to offer him the false image and show him instead the pitiful reality. Then the peace of being fully accepted comes to us in all our insufficiency. No man, however unbelieving or set in evil ways, is outside that mighty acceptance.

We hear much about the tension of present day living. Doctors, convinced of the many evils that arise from it prescribe a deliberate technique of relaxation. I suggest that the practice of acceptance is a spiritual technique even more rewarding. Once the attitude is established most of the tensions created by fear, shame and anxiety are eased and relaxed. The whole being can expand in freedom and can begin to experience the wonder and fullness of its own life as it goes out freely to all the hazards of living. It will see afresh the uniqueness of its fellows and savour their varying qualities; it will find renewed zest in the wonderful stream of happenings in which it is involved; it will even find an amused tolerance for that queer creature who goes by its own name. There is a special serenity that shines out from an 'acceptor', an absence of strain and fret, an impression of fullness of life, an outflowing of joyous energy. The forces released by the unlocking of conflicts due to shame and anxiety are now available for living and they release a harmonious vigour, a sign of a healthy personality.

CHAPTER NINE

Old and Young

A special temptation lies in wait for most elderly folk. They see the values and standards of behaviour of their own lifetime changing with the years and a new generation running out into different ways of thinking and behaving. Inevitably to the older generation the changes seem to be for the worse. We deplore the loosening of morals, the degradation of taste, the misuse of freedom and what seems to us the dangerous affluence that was unknown in our own youth. We condemn, largely because we cannot understand. It seems to us that music has become a horrid noise, painting has neither form nor beauty, poetry is obscure and lacks any appeal, while the modern novel appalls by its naif obscenity. We have outgrown our own more decorous age and are uneasy in an alien environment. We are told 'the world is for the young'.

I speak as an elderly person and I know that this is the natural way for us to react to modern developments. We cannot *understand*. Our difficulty is a real one and as far as history can tell us, it is a difficulty which has recurred with monotonous regularity in every age. How is this gap between the generations to be bridged, or is it in fact unbridgeable? Our own generation is dwindling and we are left to find our place in a strange world, a world for the young, a confusing, alarming world in which we feel useless and superfluous. To gird at this world for the young is to waste strength; we have no power to alter it. We can either condemn it and stay outside its restless orbit or we can accept it, get curious about it and at least try to understand it with sympathy. Our own attitude will largely determine the way in which this new world of the young will treat us. If we are hostile and stand aside we shall injure no one but ourselves. If we can accept it and keep an open mind, the young will accept us.

They are reluctantly aware that they have something to learn from us but they will take nothing from us if we patronise them, scold them or bore them. Too often, they regard old age as a kind of illness, a diminishment, a misfortune. That they will ever come to this themselves is unthinkable. One imagines that they will be as disconcerted as we are when their turn comes. Meanwhile, how are we to reach each other so that we may share the good things each of us holds in trust for the other? There are special blessings and insights characteristic of the young as well as of the old and they need to be shared. We think ourselves to be the experienced ones and pride ourselves on our wisdom and knowledge of life so it is surely up to us to take the initiative. How are we to set about breaking down the idea that old age is a rather sour kind of joke, a diminishment and degradation?

I suppose that the answer is that we must so live our lives as to give the lie to such ideas. This may mean a radical change in our attitude to the young. We must cease to condemn. We must accept. We must find the key to sympathy and understanding. Instead of averting our eyes we must learn to look with love. This youth that seems so hard and self-sufficing has its own poignant sorrows and fears as well as its arrogance. Indeed, may it not be that this arrogance is often just a brave attempt to outface its own insecurity? Can we feel our way into the often hurt and suffering spirits of these young people who appear so tough and self-confident? A modern writer, speaking of the storms of passion that sweep the lives of the young says: 'My heart stops when I see young people in the power of these emotions. They are so strong, so fragile, vulnerable, impermanent.'

Then too, apart from the headlong impulses of their own passions the young are increasingly bombarded by temptations. The powerful and insidious influences of the world of advertising are focused upon them. Their desires and needs are subtly excited and magnified. Against this barrage of suggestion they have no longer the steadying protection of the standard of morals that safeguarded our own impetuous youth. Who would not be afraid for them growing up so defenceless in a world organised to exploit them? Let us pause then, to think of the penalties of all these new freedoms. Our own youth was hedged in by conventions and taboos which, irksome as we may have thought them, at least saved us from the worst of our own rash impulses. These children have no such safeguards; they are at the mercy of their own passions. They are wide-open to the continual pressure of temptation from books, advertisements, cinema and television. Among themselves, no holds are barred. Can we see the perils they face without a fearful pity, can we watch their often gallant efforts without admiration, can we see their failures without sympathy?

They need our support and love and we have to make these available in an acceptable form. Too often we frustrate our own efforts to help by our half-conscious attitude of criticism. Some self-discipline will be needed before we can correct this, open our hearts to them and refuse to be hurt if our advances are not welcomed. We have to be patient and let it work. If our own attitude is right the right response will eventually come. There can be a wonderful enrichment of life for both young and old when they share their special gifts freely with each other. It is worth all the thoughtful effort we may have to make to build this bridge between the generations.

It may help us if we try to understand the illusory nature of what we call age – that seemingly accidental sequence of events that brought us into the world either before or after our friends and relatives. In what respect are we really 'older' than our grandchildren? A child can often confound its elders by suddenly turning upon them the regard of an old, old spirit full of the deep wisdom of innocence. What have I to show that proves my superiority to the child? Or, indeed, should it be the other way about? I pride myself, perhaps, on my experience of life, my knowledge of the world and of human nature, but even as I make such claims their poverty is obvious. These things, mental habits and attitudes, are not matters for pride; they are disguises I have adopted, defences I have built up, masks I wear to hide the soiling and weariness of the long journey. If there is to be any comparison between the child and an older person it must be between the essential being in each. It is only on this basis that either of us can claim an advantage. If I can succeed in coming at the shy, hidden self I have shut down under all this boasted worldly wisdom and experience, what shall I find? The essential self is perennially a child, delicate, defenceless, innocent – own brother to the child in the heart of everyman, whatever his age. Have we forgotten about this child? He is still alive within us, please God. Age is a mere accident; it is only a misfortune if it has buried our real self so deeply that we cannot get at it. When death comes so much of the extraneous quality due to our load of experience will fall away and leave exposed the child-nature which has all along been the kernel of our being. What am I doing, then, patronising these children who in reality are neither older nor younger than myself?

The idea of the unbridgeable gap between the generations is a false one. It is born of our infatuation with experience and knowingness. Whatever illusions the young may cherish (and we may have antagonised them enough to arouse strong resentment) we have no excuse for not being more clear-sighted. Our part is to find the eternal youth in ourselves and to leave it defenceless in the face of these other children. They cannot know us until we have thrown away our disguises. Their vision is obscured by these grey hairs, elderly dignity and air of authority. It is these things they resent or fear, even pity and despise. If they could see in the eyes of the greybeard the defenceless, eager, child-spirit all the trappings of age would cease to hide from them our essential kinship. We have no right to blame the young when we find ourselves described as 'fuddy-duddies'. 'poor old things', 'dead, but won't lie down'. It is our own fault. We have insisted so much on our disguise that the younger ones have accepted it as the real thing. To establish any real relationship with them we have to dare to take off the white wig and false whiskers and the looks of conscious superiority that go with them and give them a glimpse of the child within.

CHAPTER TEN

Dying

Dying is a very private experience and all the onlooker sees of it is probably misleading. We can note the failing powers, the clouded understanding, the laboured breath and the apparent agonies of dissolution, but the subjective aspect of this distressing experience cannot be known to us. It seems more than likely that death comes to the sufferer himself in a far more merciful form than we can imagine.

An understanding of the four-fold structure of this body of ours may give us a clearer picture of what happens when it disintegrates. We must remember that during sleep we have always experienced a separated being; the unconscious body on the bed is not the whole man. The higher parts of his being have lifted clear of the physical and its etheric counterpart, which, without the astral (emotional) and spiritual modes of being, can have no consciousness at all. The higher parts of the being can attain a partial consciousness in their separated state and it is a reflection of this that we are able to recall on waking in the form of a dream. Only when the four 'bodies' are again re-united does full consciousness return and we wake up and know ourselves again.* Sleeping is thus a kind of rehearsal for dying. We do not feel any fear when at night we

* see my *Fourfold Vision* for a fuller analysis.

62

abandon ourselves to unconsciousness because the experience is so familiar and we are confident that we shall wake up again in the morning in full control of our lives. We need have no more fear about our waking again when we come to die since death is only a special form of the familiar sleep process.

When death is near the two higher forms usually draw away, sometimes by easy stages as when death is preceded by senility which is caused by the incomplete union between the four 'bodies' and consequent failure of the mental powers which depend on their harmonious working together. But when death is imminent they may withdraw quite a while before the body finally gives up the struggle. The real man, in fact, has gone before his body has died. We say 'He is unconscious' and this is true since the link between the conscious self and the unconscious body is wearing thin and will soon break. The astral and spiritual forms may re-enter the body at intervals during these last days and so consciousness may be intermittent. Eventually they will find it impossible to come back and then the physical and etheric bodies will be left to finish the business alone. The physical body is in distress; it is breaking down and can no longer obey the etheric body's demands. The final separation between these two is the process which to the watcher appears to be such an agonising struggle, a desperate fight for breath. Yet the higher self with its own kind of consciousness has lifted clear of all this distress and does not feel the death-pangs which to the watcher seem so dreadful. In fact, the man has 'died' long before his body has given up the struggle. We only see the grim physical aspect of dying and it is little wonder that it leaves a frightening effect on the mind. How will it be with us when our turn comes? is the inevitable question.

I think we may take comfort in the knowledge that the actual throes of the death struggle will not be consciously experienced by us. These do not concern the essential self. It has lifted clear of the suffering body of which it is henceforth unaware. The body itself, for all its apparent distress cannot and does not have any consciousness of its own struggles. The separation protects both. Only extreme pain can rivet the higher bodies to their suffering counterpart and even this must eventually give way to oblivion. Moreover, nowadays we are mercifully able to control such acute suffering and so to ease the separation. So let us not be terrified of dying. A natural death, or death after long illness is a peaceful and unconscious process.

And what next? What of the waking? The higher forms of the man are now cut off from any return to the physical body and they have to learn to exist without their old companion, slave and sometime tyrant. The kind of consciousness to which they now have to adjust will be different because the kind of body they now inhabit will be new and strange to them. As we should expect, consciousness in this new form will at first be dreamlike. but it will gradually adjust itself to new conditions and to a keener, brighter and happier world of experience. We can only know of this world through what is told us by those who have experienced death.

In what follows I am drawing on information given me by many different communicators during half a lifetime's work as a medium. The actual experience of dying seems never to be recalled as distressing by these friends of mine, and the overall impression is of wonder and delight at the 'brave new world' opening before them. It may seem hard that life after death should not always be easy and pleasant, however doubtful the quality of our earth-life may have been. Is this reasonable? In the moment of dying shall the sinner be transformed into the saint? Life as we know it does not show us this kind of miracle, nor should we expect it to happen merely as the result of dying. If we survive death as we believe we do, it is *we* – faulty human beings – who survive and the faults we have not cured here must be endured there until we can amend them.

Here is an account of his experiences by a man who died in extreme old age after years of failing health but with his mental powers undimmed:

'I was ill for a long time with gradual weakening and finally I reached a stage where I was helpless. I slept or was unconscious most of the time. I was aware of friends and of their love and concern and I felt a vague sorrow for my wife and tried to express fears for her well-being to my son. So I left this to him and slept. I do not remember any more. I woke again but it seemed dark and quiet so I lapsed again into unconsciousness. I suppose this may have lasted for a long time but eventually I woke in bright light and feeling well and strong again. As seemed natural, I was in bed and at first I was confused and thought myself still at home. But this was a different room and there were strange faces about me. I roused and sat up and then recognised my dear sister who welcomed me and made me understand that I was safely 'dead' and that all I had dreaded was over. I soon grew strong and able to pick up the threads of new experiences. I have a great deal to learn but my body and mind are so delightfully active and joyful that every moment of living is wonderful. I wish so much that I could make this convincing to those who are still on earth, especially to my wife who may be dreading her own passing. There is nothing to fear and everything to gain.'

Here, a strong, fully matured personality has been able to set off with delight on the next stage of his journey. He is not hampered by over-much love of the life of the sensations and can happily dispense with it. He will not be hindered either by disordered or diseased emotions. His strong intellect will find new scope and power in the altered perspectives of a novel kind of consciousness.

The following account is from a younger man. He was a blunt and outspoken person, a rather tempestuous character and his 'O, blow this!' is enough to bring him vividly back to my mind. He says:

'I was so taken by surprise that you would have laughed. I went rather suddenly and it was as though I had slipped off a high precipice into a sea of sleep. I don't know how long it was before I came to and when I did I couldn't place myself at all. I was alone and on a kind of moorland and it was dim and misty. I was hazily aware that I was naked and rather hoped that no one would come along. I had not got round to the idea that I was dead because I felt so strong and well. Then I couldn't link this up with what I remembered so I thought it must be some queer kind of dream. I thought "O blow this! I'm going to sleep again", and I did. The next time I woke up there were people around and they had clothing for me and made me realise that I was really "dead". I laughed at that and said "Well if this is dying, I don't mind it a bit". They helped me to find my father and mother and later on I got in touch with your people. I forgot to say that when I woke up the second time I could see and hear quite clearly. My new friends here were very patient with me and my fits of rage and unreasonableness but of course I had to get the better of this trouble or I should not have been fit for F . . . when she came. I worried about her but somehow I knew she wouldn't be long and to my great joy she is here with me now.'

Here is a communication from a man of 65, a vigorous and energetic person of warm sympathies and affections. He died very suddenly from thrombosis. He says:

'I remember a strange feeling of tightness in my head and a blow and then no more. I was not aware of anything at all until I woke up on a hillside quite alone. I looked around and found no one so I just sat there and enjoyed the green and beautiful prospect. I was aware of a lightness and ethereality about my body. I moved it with such ease that I began to think there must be something strange about my state as there certainly was about my sitting naked on that hillside. I wasn't worried; I was far too happy and content to await developments. But I really knew then that I had died and that nevertheless all was well with me.

'I think I must have slept again. When I woke this time there was a young man, dark, with a fine face and figure and he asked my name, told me he knew of me and would bring me to friends if I would follow him. We went on together and I learnt about his connection with you. Soon we came to houses and people and I asked about J . . . and M . . . After I was equipped and ready we set out to find them. The strange thing about looking for anyone here is that one only has to think strongly enough about them and just go automatically in the direction one's footsteps take. So before long I found them in a house they had made their home and in which I was able to join them. It was a very joyful reunion. There was so much to hear and to tell.

'With this home as my base I have been exploring this wonderful new world and finding many of my old friends. It has also given me great joy to be able to find and help other friends as they have arrived here. It is too soon to make any plans or to settle to any particular job. I want to start painting again; the colours, light, vivid joy and vitality in everything are so great that I despair of being able to catch them, but it will be great fun to try. Life is going to be fuller, richer and more varied as well as being lived in another key, "revved up" as you might say, only that is to cheapen the clarity and keenness of our new way of living.'

Here is a man of courage who has known great sorrow borne without bitterness, but whose life seems to have been free from major emotional conflicts. His genial, affectionate nature, issuing in service to his fellows, and his genius for friendship will make his stay in the early planes both happy for himself and helpful to others. Significantly, he records no experience of the dark and misty interlude most communicators mention. His reference to painting, which he took up as a hobby late in life is typical of the happy amateur – painting is 'fun'.

What emerges from these accounts is the ease and naturalness of the actual passing as it is experienced by the person himself. Discomfort and pain are associated entirely with the body, and once consciousness is cut off from it the ills it has suffered are left behind and a new life opens. We are so conditioned to identifying ourselves with the body that it is difficult to view it as a sheath with which we can easily dispense. 'Shuffling off this mortal coil' seems to us on this side of death a very formidable business but in the actual event it is much less of an ordeal than we anticipate. The transition is graded too, so that there is no shock. In each account we are told of a period of sleep or of dim awareness which precedes the final awakening. The etheric form, so closely related to the physical body and only parting from it after death may linger on the earth plane for awhile and even transmit glimpses of what is happening in the death chamber or among one's friends, but these fade out and a state of sleep ushers in the full consciousness of the new world. While the etheric body remains with the surviving higher forms, it appears to slow down their rate of vibration so that the senses are not able to adjust to the new environment. Hence the interlude of misty uncertainty, almost a replica of the dream

world of ordinary sleep, also due to dissociated
modes of being.

This state of things passes as soon as the etheric
body is shed, which appears to happen during the
period of sleep. Then one awakens to a bright and
clearly-seen world. The new senses function nor-
mally, the new body is alert and vigorous and so
surprisingly light and easy to move that mere
existence is pure joy.

For the sake of completeness, I include the
description of a passing complicated by the shock
of a violent death. The communicator had come to a
nihilistic view of existence and the end had overtaken
him in a mood of reckless despair. His experience is
not typical but represents the maximum difficulty in
adjustment. Here was a complex and unhappy mind,
torn by inner conflicts and shaken by despair. The
shock of a violent death accentuated his difficulties.
He had crashed on a motor cycle and had died
after lying in a coma for some days. He says:

'The grey road rose swiftly to meet me and a
shattering blow put me out. Immeasurable time
seemed to pass before I came to myself without the
accompaniment of pain. Then I opened my eyes
with a shock of surprise because somewhere in my
mind was the conviction that I could neither move
nor see, but the nightmare had lifted and I opened
unbandaged eyes. I raised a hand to feel my head
and was reassured. The last half-hour terminating in
the crash had retreated into a misty past and I lay
and contemplated the small distant views of road-
sides reeling past, grey skies and spring blur of
hedgerows. There had been an accident in which I

had been knocked out. I ought then, to be in bed somewhere, perhaps in a hospital. Soon I should wake up from what must be a dream and find myself there. But here I felt again at my head; no bandage, no injury, no bed. Around me was a misty shroud of opaqueness which might have been a sea-fog. Moreover, I was actually lying there entirely uncovered yet not in the least chilled or uncomfortable. It seemed a happy and natural thing to be thus and I was free from pain and quite unconcerned over my plight. But the connection with all the past content of my mind refused to be made. I had been, and I was, but between the two states there was an enigmatic gap.

'I slept and woke several times before the suggestion that I was actually 'dead' occurred to me and even then it was some time before I forced myself to entertain it. The cheerful earth had vanished completely but there was the undoubted fact of my own very vital continuance. For I was more than merely alive in an earth sense; I was thrillingly, tensely alive with all my being accentuated, keyed up and emotionally charged as never before. My body was actual, yet weight and solidity had gone, movement no longer lifted inertial mass but was the thing it moved. Somewhere my body must be lying smashed and to all appearance dead. It was perhaps in a hospital ward and there must be people about. Then I had slipped out of that and was here, yet *here* was actually *there* since I had not moved. Could I by any chance see into that lost world? Confused glimpses of it, friends there, relatives too, within touch, yet for ever beyond my calling, They looked at the broken body on the bed and thought . . .? I wondered to what blissful heaven of their own imagining they had consigned me when I was still there in their midst. Great billows of emotion assailed me; sorrow flooded into me from all around.'

The world in which this communicator wandered for some time had a shifting, blurred character more dreamlike than a dream. He felt the influence of brooding presences but saw nothing in this foggy flat arena of consciousness. He was still very near the earth-sphere and it was some time before the chaotic condition of his emotional body cleared so that he was able to see and feel the new environment as it really was, and to find his way into happier surroundings.* Much undoubtedly depends on the state of the emotional body before death. If this is healthy and vigorous one is ready to go straight on rejoicing into the world of light. Where development is poor or chaotic, as in the above account, souls may wander in this dim world of misty outlines for some time. It would seem that the environment is there in all its clear beauty, but that the senses are undeveloped and so interpret it in terms of their own blindness.

Another common element in the accounts I have quoted is the rather disconcerting absence of clothing. But what can one expect? 'Naked came I into the world, and naked I shall go out of it.' Those who make it their business to help the newly arrived are provided against this necessity and the difficulty is quickly solved. The need for help sends out its

---

* For his full story see *Post Mortem Journal*

summons and one is quickly found and cared for. The novel sense of vitality and well-being makes one almost oblivious to such an unimportant detail as nakedness; prudishness is left behind with the body.

As soon as the new senses are well established, the new environment has a reassuring stability. It is as actual in the features of the landscape as the familiar earth. Hills, valleys, woods and rivers are just as real and far more vividly beautiful. To quote from another informant:

'Your consciousness of solidity and mass are the effects of senses especially adjusted to a physical world. We now have senses adjusted equally well to a world of etheric matter. So of course this is relatively as actual to us as the world we have left.'

Accounts of the new environment agree in essentials but one must expect wide differences in detail since one chooses one's surroundings according to inclinations formed during earth life. Thus, to the confirmed town dweller, country life would be uncongenial so he will make his home among the crowded streets of a city. The kind of city even will depend on his tastes either for grandeur or for a more humble kind of life. He may, it is true, outgrow his earlier choice. The country-lover will choose to live among hills and woods and will find beauty there of an unearthly kind. Wherever one's inclinations lead there will be found an added zest, an almost magic vitality in the people, the animals and the plants. It is, of course, the heightening of the vital principle in oneself which makes experience so joyful and full of meaning. To quote again:

'One of the first impressions the newcomer gets is

of the wonderful ease and lightness of movement, a
feeling of such springing vigour that one can hardly
stay on the ground. It is difficult to recall the heavy
weight of an earth-body and the dragging effort of
moving it about. Aches and pains and stiffness are
unbelievable. As to our matter, the lowest kind
corresponding to your mineral matter, is etheric in
nature. There are several grades of this progressing
up to the astral substance of which our bodies are
made. Again, astral matter ranges through several
ascending degrees fining out into the beginning of
the spiritual, which to us takes the form of light.
In this new life none of the necessities of comfortable living are absent. It is a great mistake to think
of this present stage of our living as quite ethereal
and no longer dependent on comforts. We still have
bodies and they have their needs. But there are
great differences for all that. On earth you feel heat
and cold but neither are known here. We have no
darkness and no division into day or night. You can
reckon up the many things we do not need in con-
sequence. No fires, no cooking, no cumbersome
clothing, no artificial lighting all of which to a
housewife is a great release. I must explain about
food. When one first comes eating is a habit as well
as a pleasure of the senses. But the senses you
gratify by eating are dependent upon your etheric
body and when this is shed only the emotions which
have become connected with eating and drinking
remain. These may at first induce a craving for
remembered pleasure and so food may be eaten.
There is plenty of an insubstantial kind of food
to be got and it is usually the newcomers who are

unable to do without it. One may, of course, bring over appetites and cravings that are unhealthy and unwise, but at first it may be right to indulge them. Very soon the tendency corrects itself as one's astral body gets clear of its ailments.

'Although we have no day or night, we quite often feel the need for a break in active life and then we go apart and rest. I used to drop off into a kind of half-sleep mostly from old habit I think, but the need rapidly decreases. You may think such a life sounds like an unbearable strain but the difference in the quality of our bodies and their capacity for continuous effort makes it quite natural.'

In all these descriptions of the near-earth planes of being we seem to be shown a mercifully graded ascent, as though our human weaknesses and needs are to be tolerated and not condemned until such time as we have outgrown them. Other and more serious aspects of our failings there are and we have to see, understand and correct them before we can go on. But all these things are an accompaniment to reunion with our friends and the gladness of a more bountiful life. The loving purpose that wills our progress to full maturity may surely be trusted to guide us safely through the difficulties. As one of our communicators said 'There is nothing to fear, and everything to gain'.

CHAPTER ELEVEN

Meeting and Parting

If we accept survival of death we naturally think of rejoining the friends who have preceded us. Shall we find them again unaltered and shall we be able to take up again the same affectionate relationship?

There are no easy answers to such questions although the evidence we have is reassuring. We are told that relationships after death are based on the principle of affinity, which is experienced as distance, so that we find ourselves near in space to those with whom we have this real relationship of quality and separated by space from those with whom we have no real ties. So we have to ask ourselves whether we were really related to our friends in this inescapable fashion, or was our earthly tie just a matter of propinquity or convenience? If it had no more reality than this or if it had not stood the testing of time and circumstances, then we cannot expect that it will continue into this new world where shams are unthinkable. We can be sure that our friends with whom there has been a really strong bond of love and understanding will find us and that we shall come together in a joy far greater than we can now envisage. There will be many new friends too, for like draws to like regardless of previous rank or class, age, sex or nationality.

We need to be realists in our appraisal of our

closest relationships. The word 'love' has been so distorted among us that one almost hesitates to use it. What we call by that name is seldom free from self-regard and possessiveness and it can mask lust, or the vanity that needs to be fed by adoration, or even a greedy desire to possess and dominate. We make promises of eternal fidelity far too readily here, and often find that they cannot be kept even for the short term of our earth-life. Incompatibilities develop and early rapture fades into indifference. Such marriages are kept in being only from a sense of duty and they are in truth 'until death us do part', for death will effectually separate the two who have no real affinity with each other; they are henceforth free from the coercion of the vows made so recklessly on earth.

But where there has been a deep attachment and the love between the partners has been a selfless devotion they will inevitably find each other again. We can rely securely on the tie of affinity which will need no reinforcement from formal vows. We are apt to forget that when one partner of such a united couple dies he or she will suffer from the separation as much as the one who is left on earth. The one who has died, however, has the advantage of the knowledge of survival and that only a few short years of separation may have to be faced.

Our short views of life, bounded by the few brief decades of our earth life, confuse the issue for us. This is only an episode in our long pilgrimage. We have further to go than we realised and our companions on the journey will be those with whom we have close and real ties. Who knows to what distant heights his spirit may eventually climb? Who knows what exalted companions he may find on the journey? One thing alone is certain. Where there has been pure and selfless love it cannot be lost. It is the highest activity of the eternal part of the man, and as such it shares in his immortality. It confers perfect freedom yet is the unbreakable bond of permanent union. If our earthly relationships approximate to this standard we need have no fear.

The thought of some loved friend, husband, wife, mother or brother often comes comfortingly to the dying and there is a hope and expectation of meeting them again. This may be helpful when we wake in our new condition because the strong expectation will probably alert the friend and bring him to our aid. We can, it seems, trust to an automatic sense of direction which will take us towards our desire, so if there is an ardent wish to meet a particular person we shall be guided towards him. So much of our present fear of strangeness and loneliness is due to our physical bodies which isolate us from each other. In our new life we can communicate with each other so much more freely; the barrier of the flesh has gone and we can dispense with the words which so often cause misunderstanding and confusion. We see and know our friends in immediate awareness and the sense of 'togetherness' and the closeness of communion must be a source of the keenest joy. So the fears of loneliness, and of being misunderstood are things of the past.

What can we do here and now to prepare for these novel conditions? We can take a closer look at the network of relationships we have made here;

we can re-examine them in the light of reality and be completely candid with ourselves. How many of these ties will persist when accidents of kinship and propinquity are removed? In view of the keener nature of the emotions we shall feel there, we need to revise our conventional views of the claims of love. In fact, we have to realise that a pure love *makes* no claims. It sets the object of its love free even from its own needs. If we scrutinise our relationship with those near and dear to us we shall almost certainly discover a possessive jealousy making anxious claims on a devotion regarded as a right. Here then, in the intimacy of our closest relationships is a field of work where we may do much to purify our emotions, recognising their baser elements and doing our best to clear them. If we take jealousy and possessiveness with us when we die our friends will almost certainly escape us. Only genuine unselfish love will have the right to survive. We shall do well to remove as many barriers as we can between ourselves and those whose love we prize, so that we may find again after death the joy of a true kinship and may know each other in that which is eternal.

CHAPTER TWELVE

The New Body

We have been told of the sensation of lightness and ease which immediately makes itself felt when we eventually wake up in our new world. Our body, the body which is so like the physical form we have left behind us, is now the astral or emotional form which, although it has always been the driving force of our active lives on earth, has only been able to express itself through the cumbersome mechanisms of the flesh. Now it is free of them and its volatile, urgent nature has direct expression. The state of this radiant new body of ours is now clearly to be seen in its changing light and colour. Every passing emotion stirs and varies its appearance and betrays the living truth of our nature. No concealment is possible now. We can no longer practice insincerity or hide hostility with a polite smile or make use of false words of reassurance. Whether we have been habitually honest or not, honesty now is unavoidable.

I suppose we are most of us unconscious of the small insincerities of our daily intercourse, of the reservations of truth and even of the insidious factual truth-speaking which may mask an actual lie. Such practices now will be apparent as sullyings of our brightness, as a dimming of the purity of our colour. Anger now cannot be hidden under a calm countenance for a dart of flame will be seen, and will be felt as a burning pain by those towards whom it is directed. If we are frightened, our fear will surround us like a choking fog and disgust will stream out as a bilious yellow mist. All the negative emotions will make us disgusting to ourselves and abhorrent to our friends who may have to give us a wide berth until we are cured of these ailments; for now our faults of temper are felt as physical illnesses needing a physician.

On the other hand, happy emotions will radiate out from us to bless all who come near us. They will be seen as brilliant light and shimmering colours of the utmost beauty, and their effects on others will be healing and stimulating. For all these now-tangible emotions will be absorbed by the sensitive bodies of those we meet. The intensity of our own happiness can only be imagined in our present dim lethargic state. The emotions we feel now, however powerful they seem to be, are dulled by the interposition of the flesh. When this no longer shields us all our life of feeling will be keener and more powerful, free from restraint and perhaps difficult to keep under control. As one communicator says:

'All experiences now are tried out on the quick of the being and in their piercing reality are beyond anything it is possible to feel on earth. My emotions still shake me dangerously and I have to learn also to take the emotional impact of others with equanimity. I have become wary of impatience or anger; their manifestations are too repulsive.'

So for passionate and undisciplined natures the early stages of adaptation to this more fluid body are not easy. The cure of long-standing emotional illnesses must first be undergone before one can take one's proper place among one's peers. Fortunately there are devoted souls, doctors of the spirit, who make the healing mission their own.

Enough has been said to warn us to take ourselves in hand here and now and to improve our emotional condition while we still have the merciful shield of the body to protect us from its full effect. If we harbour resentments or suspicions, or are prey to anxieties, jealousies or fears we should realise that to take these with us unaltered is to ensure for ourselves a kind of purgatory. Even a grief we have kept alive when we should have outgrown it may cause us great suffering. Again, one can understand some of the apparently harsh sayings of Jesus in this light as metaphors for the difficult process of cure. Even those of us who seem to be untroubled by the more obvious emotional diseases, whose lives appear placid and serene, may find we have hidden troubles which need dealing with.

This is to stress the negative side; if the sorrows are more poignant, so the loving kindness is more radiant and the fun and laughter more enchanting. Love sends out its healing rays of such fine and intense vibration that they can overrule and harmonise the jarring disharmonies of the negative emotions and in the long run it cannot fail to cure all the diseases of the soul. If we could only *see* it operating here, as we shall do there, we should realise what a power for good it is and how it blesses and heals even under earth-conditions. But it works effectively even here although to us it works invisibly. We can do a great deal for others in this way and we can by the same means clear up our own disharmonies. The important thing is to realise the practical urgency of this, in view of its effect on our new bodies. Our life of feeling is not just a matter of inward experience private to ourselves but the only aspect of our being which will survive death in a visible form. We have just a little time to remake this vital new body of ours.

The early stages of life after death are mainly concerned with clearing and purifying the new body and curing its diseases. Yet this does not go on in a vacuum. We are soon absorbed into a vivid life of relationships, some with old friends new-found, some with new friends. We lead lives of pleasant activities of work and play in lovely surroundings and it is in this setting that our task of cleansing and rehabilitating the earth-soiled emotional body goes on. We are helped both by professional doctors and by our friends who themselves have had to undergo similar cures when they first came.

The whole of our earth experience with its joys and sorrows, its tensions and difficulties, its opportunities taken and its failures mourned: all this has formed and moulded our new body. We have made it ourselves, marred and imperfect as it may be. When we see it as it really is we shall have a measure of the true value of our life. This is the moment of truth, the real 'Day of Judgement', no external day of wrath, but a judgement of the self, by the self. It may well be the day when 'the last shall be first, and the first last', for many earthly judgements of worth may then be reversed.

CHAPTER THIRTEEN

In His Will is Our Peace

In all this interaction between the ageing body and the striving spirit, our concern is that the decay of the one should not deny the growth of the other. Like Plato's prisoners in the cave taking shadows for reality, we have it in our power to leave the illusions behind and come forth into the sunshine. Everyday we have to resist the tyranny of the body which seeks to drag us down with its weariness and to insist on the shining energy of our still-youthful spirit so that all the suggestions of decay and dissolution are known to be illusions. It is good sometimes to turn from our own individual preoccupations and to consider the human story of which we are only an inconsiderable part.

Perhaps today mankind is about halfway on its long journey towards full development. Unconsciously, we think of ourselves as having reached full development but if we look back over the long ages of our evolutionary progress we must agree that we have no right to think ourselves the final outcome of the process. There are many reasons to think otherwise. We see through the mists of prehistory the long ages of emergence, the man-creature gradually taking on the qualities we regard as human – intelligence, memory and purpose. As he uses these he creates in himself a new centre of life, the dawning of the spirit. This will be from henceforth the urgent growing point of his being. A new awareness of himself and of his world comes to him; he sees a new heaven and a new earth. His heaven is filled with awesome presences, his earth takes on clearer meaning, sometimes glorious, sometimes sinister. He is conscious now in himself of a new tension between the new self and the strong, dark tides of animal instinct he has brought with him from the past. Out of this tension comes his sense of guilt, of shortcoming, strong in proportion to his sense of high destiny. The inner knowledge that he has far to go has drawn him on and upward and it continues to impel us onward today.

It is this inner growth, the thrust of urgent new life from within, which is our best guarantee of survival. Newly unfolding life has its imperative claim to air, space and conditions of hope. The law of growth is universal and not to be thwarted for long by any untoward circumstance. If we look around us with seeing eyes, the law of inevitable growth may take on for us the unfailing and inexorable expression of the will of God. It is plain to read in the face of all creation. Feeling within us, too, this strong movement of new life, this potentiality for endless growth, we may know that this is something over which death can have no power. We trust in the assurance of this irresistible urge for fuller, freer life, and I am convinced that we do not trust in vain.

Death will come, then, not as a foe but as a friend. To those who are conscious of the demand of their spirit to live and grow, death will be the opener of the prison door, the angel of deliverance who will strike

85

off our chains and lead us out into the sunshine of freedom. Life has been good, earth has been beautiful, love has been richly ours, but the embryo spirit is urgent to be reborn and its claims to live and grow need other air, other earth, other skies.

'Hast loved fair eyes and lips of gentle
   breath?
Fade then and fall, thou hast had all
That life can give; ask somewhat
   now of death.'*

In all our wayward, heedless life, turning over its treasures, spending and wasting its opportunities, using or refusing its gifts, we have known hours of joy and of rich satisfaction, hours, too, of discouragement, disillusion and dismay. Looking back, we may be able to trace a pattern in all this, a connection between the good hours and our harmony with the good, and the unhappy ones when we were rebelling against that harmony. Our peace has depended, far more than we have known, on working with, rather than against the creative love which moves in and through all things. Now as the evening closes in we are learning to accept: our world with all its strife and perplexity, our friends with all their enriching differences, even ourselves in all our weakness and failure. 'In His will is our peace' say the humble souls in the lowest circle of Dante's *Paradise*. So through experience of beauty, love, pain and death we too may come to this highest wisdom.

No story, no great music, no poem could have form or purpose unless it was confined within the limits of beginning and end. Our human story, too,

---

* Richard Garnet, *Fading Leaf and Fallen Leaf*.

must have its closing here or it would lack significant form. How should the full story develop if this chapter were not to end? So the chronicle of our earthly days is nearing its end; the climax is past, the interest waning. Death must turn the page, and shall we try to stay his hand?

The vision of a future life, no paradisal dream of soft felicity but an inspiring and purposeful growth towards fulfilment shines beyond the twilight of our days. Rest for the weary, yes. Rest for as long as it is needed. Beyond that it would become boredom. But as the weariness of earth passes from us, we shall go on into the world of light. Here we shall find that fullness of life that we have glimpsed but never properly experienced on earth. 'The kingdom, the power and the glory' are there. Every step of our journey towards them can be irradiated with their joy. From time to time we may have divine foretastes of their blessedness, for heaven can be here and now, as well as hereafter.

'So at the last shall come old age . . .
And then, as, mid the dark, a gleam
Of yet another morning breaks,
And like the hand that ends a dream,
Death, with the might of his sunbeam
Touches the flesh and the soul awakes.'*

* Browning, *The flight of the Duchess*.